ROB'S WORD SHOP

Robert Fitterman

Archive & Afterword
by Lawrence Giffin

Rob's Word Shop
Copyright (c) Robert M. Fitterman, 2019

Additional materials provided by Records Manager Lawrence Giffin

Rob's Word Shop would like to acknowledge the following individuals and institutions for their support of this project:

The Bowery Poetry Club, Mildred's Lane, Woodstock Digital Media Festival (2012), *OnandOn Screen*, and *Dear Navigator*. Special thanks to Records Manager Lawrence Giffin, for his assistance to the shop and his many hours of transcription. Thanks, also, to Steve Giasson who assisted with the transcription.

Finally, thanks to the Rob's Word Shop customers.

....

First Edition, 2019
ISBN 978-1-937027-48-3

Ugly Duckling Presse
The Old American Can Factory
232 Third Street #E-303
Brooklyn, NY 11215
www.uglyducklingpresse.org

Distributed by Small Press Distribution

Designed by Don't Look Now! in collaboration with the author
Typeset in Optima

Printed in Latvia by Jelgavas Tipografija

Of seven-hundred and fifty copies printed, the first seventy-five are numbered and signed by both the Proprietor and the Records Manager of Rob's Word Shop.

Contents

DAY 1 …………………………… *10*

DAY 2 …………………………… *24*

DAY 3 …………………………… *52*

DAY 4 …………………………… *54*

DAY 5 …………………………… *68*

DAY 6 …………………………… *88*

DAY 7 …………………………… *90*

DAY 8 …………………………… *126*

DAY 9 …………………………… *144*

DAY 10 …………………………… *158*

DAY 11 …………………………… *172*

APPENDIX ………………………… *225*

On Wednesday, May 5th, 2010, I opened Rob's Word Shop — a storefront shop where individual letters and words were sold. The words and letters were either chosen by the individual customers or arrived at with my assistance. I would then hand-write or type the letter, word, or words. Single letters were sold for 50¢ and words for $1. My shop location was 308 Bowery (the south window at the Bowery Poetry Club), and my hours of operation were Tuesday through Thursday 11:00 AM—2:00 PM, from May 5 through May 27. As the sole proprietor of the store, I simply spread the word of my shop and opened my business to the public. Over the course of my business run, about 40 customers visited the shop. Nearly all of these exchanges were recorded as videos and can be viewed on YouTube—"robs word shop." These video conversations were then edited and transcribed for this book. Following the transcribed exchanges is an essay I commissioned from Records Manager Lawrence Giffin, and a sampling from the materials he collected for the store's archives.

DAY 1

Ledger

Left apartment at 10 AM. Picked up computer printer from friend's house at 10:15. Took taxi to 308 Bowery ($4.50) and arrived at 10:45. Set up printer, completed signage, and opened at 11:00 AM. Customer 1 arrived at 11:10 as a couple. Together they ordered a combination of single words, multiple words, and letters for a total of $26.00. The words and phrases they purchased were:

> goat
> Heather Christle
> THE SEASIDE!
> Minutes
> BOOKS
> Walser & Company
> The Robert Walser Society of Western Massachusetts
> Factory Hollow
> Flying Object (I erroneously wrote Flying Sobject, and offered it free of charge)
> Flying Subject
> FLYING OBJECT
> FLYING SUBJECT

The recording did not work for Customer 1, so unfortunately there is no transcript of the conversation.

Customer 2 arrived around 11:50AM. This customer purchased 2 words for $2: interpolation and selfhood.

Customer 2A arrived at 1:30 and purchased 1 word for $1: escape. This customer sought consultation in choosing her word. She was a journalist who happened upon the store and requested not to be recorded. Closed the shop at 2:00 PM. Walked home and arrived at 2:15 PM.

Total sales: $29.00.

Customer 1

[No transcript or video due to technical difficulties. The above words from the ledger were sold for a total of $26.00.]

Customer 2

ROB: what's it going to be?

CUSTOMER 2: interpolation

ROB: you're getting a lot for your money on that one... ok, good

CUSTOMER 2: wait, how much is it?

ROB: it's one dollar a word

CUSTOMER 2: oh good, oh good... should I pay in advance like with a manicure?

ROB: no, nope... you don't have to pay in advance... would you like that handwritten or...?

CUSTOMER 2: yep

ROB: ok... I like...

CUSTOMER 2: ...in cursive

ROB: I'm enjoying the handwritten...

CUSTOMER 2: yeah

ROB: ...in cursive

CUSTOMER 2: in cursive with that... do you have a thick felt pen?

ROB: I have a pen

CUSTOMER 2: like a Sharpie?

ROB: ...and a Sharpie

CUSTOMER 2: yeah, a Sharpie

ROB: Sharpie... it's gonna be...

CUSTOMER 2: that's ok, I think...

ROB: yeah?

CUSTOMER 2: ...it could go horizontally

ROB: right... all right... see now these are all choices that...

CUSTOMER 2: ...now do you have a dictionary because I'm not exactly sure how... I'm a terrible speller

ROB: I don't

CUSTOMER 2: ok

ROB: uh, in-ter-po-late

CUSTOMER 2: pa-late... I'm not sure if it's p-a-l-l-a

ROB: p-o

CUSTOMER 2: ...or p-o

ROB: terp-o

CUSTOMER 2: no

ROB: yeah it is

CUSTOMER 2: I think it's p-a

ROB: no it's not inter-pa... it's inter-po-late... yeah

CUSTOMER 2: no 'cause you interpalate with an *a*

13

ROB: ok... well...

CUSTOMER 2: should we look it up in the dictionary?

ROB: yeah

CUSTOMER 2: we have to stop the video... no, maybe not

ROB: I don't think we do have to stop the video

CUSTOMER 2: oh... there's no wifi

ROB: yeah there is

CUSTOMER 2: ...not working

ROB: yeah

CUSTOMER 2: I don't know if Bob is charging for it

ROB: no [laughs]

CUSTOMER 2: it's not free... oh, here we go, ok, I got it

ROB: is it letting... it's still filming you while this happens?

CUSTOMER 2: no unfortunately... interpolation you're right

ROB: told ya

CUSTOMER 2: inter-po-la-tion... ok

ROB: all right, good, now let's see about... keep... while you have that in your mind let's see about the video... is it gone?

CUSTOMER 2: no it's still on... I... I put it back

ROB: yeah and you're still there? ok, great

CUSTOMER 2: mm-hmm

ROB: so, initial cap or all lowercase?

CUSTOMER 2: all lowercase but elegant cursive

ROB: elegant cursive and it'll be kinda large with the...

CUSTOMER 2: ...that's ok

ROB: ok, mm-hmm

CUSTOMER 2: not a large word... I don't like the word large

ROB: ok

CUSTOMER 2: [laughs] that's good... are you going to tattoo them too?

ROB: no... in-ter-po-late

CUSTOMER 2: two i's... I believe

ROB: no... one i

CUSTOMER 2: I don't think so

ROB: interpolator... is that what you want?

CUSTOMER 2: no... -olation, interpolation

ROB: interpolation, oh then it's two maybe

CUSTOMER 2: yeah?

ROB: two i's?

CUSTOMER 2: do you want me to look it up again?

ROB: mm-hmm... misspellings, misspellings are ok too

CUSTOMER 2: ok

ROB: it's up to you, your word

CUSTOMER 2: in-ter, in-ter-po-... no you're right, one i

ROB: mm-hmm

CUSTOMER 2: ok

ROB: you're doing well so far...

CUSTOMER 2: yeah

ROB: ...in my store, in terms of...

CUSTOMER 2: ...being um...

ROB: inter-po-la-tion, is that what we said?

CUSTOMER 2: mm-hmm

ROB: in-ter-po-la- ...tion

CUSTOMER 2: ok

ROB: how is that?

CUSTOMER 2: great

ROB: does that look ok?

CUSTOMER 2: that looks really good

ROB: ok, now why this word?

CUSTOMER 2: oh! um, well it's a word that's been on my mind in terms of... 'cause I'm in the middle of my working day and I ran over here and, um, there's a really complex set of facts and factors in some of the narratives I'm hearing and I'm thinking of my own sets of factors that I want to add to that and so this is a word that popped out

ROB: terrific... would you like it signed, or?...

CUSTOMER 2: of course

ROB: on front or back?

CUSTOMER 2: back please

ROB: ok now, um, we'll give it the stamp... would you like a stamp?

CUSTOMER 2: yeah, definitely

ROB: ...and then we're going to have a stamp on the receipt as well?

CUSTOMER 2: ok... can you sign inside the stamp?

ROB: mm-hmm... now, see, for the first customer, I didn't realize that... that wasn't really much of an option to actually stamp and sign so...

CUSTOMER 2: I think...

ROB: they didn't have that option...

CUSTOMER 2: well I think you... I think you should do that to finish it off

ROB: but I think this is . . .

CUSTOMER 2: you should decide... you should... that should be the... like when stores put a seal on it

ROB: mm-hmm

CUSTOMER 2: that... you shouldn't... that shouldn't be an option

ROB: I get that

CUSTOMER 2: that should be how you finish it off

ROB: that's an interesting thought

CUSTOMER 2: ...and I would date it... I mean I would like mine dated

ROB: all right

CUSTOMER 2: cinco de mayo

ROB: that's right, um...

CUSTOMER 2: which is five five [laughs]

ROB: I didn't realize I was opening on cinco de mayo

CUSTOMER 2: yeah, that's nice

ROB: ok

CUSTOMER 2: you should have some Spanish words

ROB: so now, um, I'll give you a receipt

CUSTOMER 2: ok, well, I should pay you

ROB: yep

CUSTOMER 2: [laughs] wow I feel like I'm getting such a deal

ROB: you are getting a good deal... so in this case we have one word...

CUSTOMER 2: yeah

ROB: one word and, um, that amount is one dollar... that's one dollar no tax, and you get the stamp again

CUSTOMER 2: oh, I need to order another word too

ROB: for the future?

CUSTOMER 2: for, uh, Coco

ROB: all right, here's the receipt for that one

CUSTOMER 2: oh, nice

ROB: mm-hmm

CUSTOMER 2: thanks

ROB: you're welcome... all right?

CUSTOMER 2: right... you should put the date on it

ROB: ok

CUSTOMER 2: I mean, I would like the date, not "you should"…

ROB: all right

CUSTOMER 2: thank you

ROB: there's the date, mm-hmm… now, um, anything else you'd like to…

CUSTOMER 2: one word, you wanna put… can you put… how many letters: one word, dot-dot-dot letters

ROB: ok

CUSTOMER 2: …in my receipt?

ROB: thirteen letters… that might be a record… I mean, so far, for today

CUSTOMER 2: do I get… do I get something if I have the most letters in my word for the day?

ROB: maybe at the end of the month… I'll have to think about that

CUSTOMER 2: should… are you gonna have a big business card-like goblet, people drop their business cards and if they have the most letters…?

ROB: that's a good idea… I'll have to think about that

CUSTOMER 2: ok… so, um, then I'd like to commission a word for Coco, and the word is selfhood

ROB: all right, so we're gonna do that in a similar way?

CUSTOMER 2: do I get a bag or folder or something?

ROB: uh, you know, I don't have any bags

CUSTOMER 2: ok… I think folders to keep it…

ROB: I'm gonna have to get some folders

CUSTOMER 2: yeah

ROB: all right, ok

CUSTOMER 2: I don't wanna, um, I don't want to fold it

ROB: ok, I need folders, all right, um, I mean, you could take some extra pieces of paper...

CUSTOMER 2: no, no... I just don't want to fold it, but...

ROB: ...do you want a rubber band?

CUSTOMER 2: oh, that's a good idea... oh yeah, you could roll 'em... I'll put 'em together

ROB: I'll do that... I'll, uh, I'll, I'll roll 'em up for you... I'm very good at that...

CUSTOMER 2: ok

ROB: it's my job...

CUSTOMER 2: ...and it's in your heritage

ROB: that's right

CUSTOMER 2: ok

ROB: ok... video's still going?

CUSTOMER 2: yep

ROB: all right

CUSTOMER 2: ok so, um, next word...

ROB: yeah

CUSTOMER 2: selfhood

ROB: selfhood

CUSTOMER 2: yeah, I think it should be one word

ROB: yeah

CUSTOMER 2: I think it should be kinda block mini caps

ROB: all caps?

CUSTOMER 2: all caps but…

ROB: small?

CUSTOMER 2: …small

ROB: also long-ways?

CUSTOMER 2: yeah

ROB: middle of the page?

CUSTOMER 2: yeah… now what would it cost if I wanted you to do that three times on the same page? three dollars?

ROB: mm-hmm

CUSTOMER 2: ok… I'll have to think about that… is there gonna be a sale?

ROB: I've considered it… I don't know

CUSTOMER 2: [laughs] it should probably open first

ROB: now is that the idea?

CUSTOMER 2: oh that's really good

ROB: is that good?

CUSTOMER 2: yeah, uh-huh

ROB: ok… beautiful word

CUSTOMER 2: yeah, yeah…

ROB: and why did you go with the all caps for this one?

CUSTOMER 2: um, well, it's an important word, it's a striking word, it's a word that needs to be, uh, forcefully written... like interpolation is more a vagary, though it's a set medical concept, it's more interpretive... this is... selfhood is selfhood... it's solid... it should be, and it's what I hope it can be for our child

ROB: that sounds good to me... very nice

CUSTOMER 2: yeah, very nice

ROB: beautiful word

CUSTOMER 2: ok, thanks... oh, I have to pay you

ROB: mm-hmm

Customer 2A

[Upon request from the customer, no video or written record is available. Customer 2A was a curious journalist who happened in to the shop off the street. We decided on a single word together: escape. The word was written with a black Sharpie in cursive, lower-case, centered in the middle of the page.]

DAY 2

Ledger

Left apartment on bicycle at 10:30 AM. Stopped at stationary store for envelopes and folders ($5.25). Arrived at Rob's Word Shop promptly at 11:00 AM. First customer arrived at 12:30 PM. Served 6 customers continuously from 12:45 to 2:05 PM. Closed shop and left 308 Bowery at 2:15 PM. Arrived at apartment, on bicycle, at 2:30 PM.

Total sales: $7.00.

Below is a list of words sold:

Customer 3	tops
Customer 4	technicolor
Customer 5	better
Customer 6	unscripted and off the books (gratis)
Customer 7	Constraint-B
Customer 8	nachleben

Customers 3, 4, 5

ROB: ok

CUSTOMER 3: ok

CUSTOMER 4: yay

ROB: does that work?

CUSTOMER 4: yeah

ROB: you're all there

CUSTOMER 3: it works

ROB: good… so, um… here are your choices: buy a word for one dollar or a letter for fifty cents and you can have me write them with either, um, a pen or a marker on a piece of paper, or we can do it on the printer… um, so you can have it computer-generated printed, or handwritten… your… whatever your letters or your word… um, so you can start thinking about words but also some customers already have a word in mind, um, I see you have a credit card…

CUSTOMER 4: oh it's my NYU ID

ROB: I'm thinking…

CUSTOMER 3: campus cash?

CUSTOMER 4: yeah, can I…?

ROB: [laughs]… you, you can't get an NYU discount unfortunately… um… so some people have an idea of what they want very specifically, uh, some people have no idea and we've discussed it together, um, some choices could be: you could come up with a word yourself, I could help you with a word, you could choose a word from this room, there's a lot of words in this room, um, or a letter, or, you know, whatever you want…

CUSTOMER 4: sweet

ROB: ...and then you get a, um, you get a receipt and you get a, uh, folder or envelope to take it away

CUSTOMER 3: oooh...

CUSTOMER 4: oooh...

CUSTOMER 3: packaging...

ROB: so anyone have a feeling first?

CUSTOMER 4: I think I'm going to do the word technicolor

ROB: the word technicolor

CUSTOMER 4: yeah

ROB: beautiful... the actual word?

CUSTOMER 4: yeah

ROB: 'cause, see, that could be a description of how you want the word

CUSTOMER 4: that's true

ROB: technicolor... ok great, so... [off] hi! are you here for the word shop?

UNIDENTIFIED CUSTOMER [OFF]: um... I'm here for the word store

ROB: the word store, yeah

UNIDENTIFIED CUSTOMER [OFF]: is it still open?

ROB: yeah, yeah, it's open... yeah, yeah... yeah... so, so... beautiful... ok... so I'm gonna take care of these customers, and then, um, we're on... techni-color, ok, good, wow, is technicolor gonna be, um, with a marker, a pen, or computer?

CUSTOMER 4: the marker

ROB: all right... the marker, beautiful, and, um, cursive or printed?

CUSTOMER 4: hmm... I guess cursive

ROB: cursive, I love that... all right, now why cursive do you think?

CUSTOMER 4: I don't know, I just think it will look more elegant

ROB: mm-hmm

CUSTOMER 4: yeah

ROB: ok.... very good... um, initial cap or no caps or all caps?

CUSTOMER 4: no caps

ROB: no caps, all right, good... lowercase technicolor... medium? big? small?

CUSTOMER 4: um... maybe like enough to take up like the middle part of the page...

ROB: the middle part, ok? and...

CUSTOMER 4: ...'cause it's kinda long

ROB: and landscape... you want it landscape?

CUSTOMER 4: yeah

ROB: we got it... I think we got it... tech-na-color... like that size?

CUSTOMER 4: yeah

ROB: looks right? did I spell that right? you never know, things look so kind of...

CUSTOMER 4: I think it's an i...

ROB: tech-nigh-color?

CUSTOMER 4: it's like tech-ni-color, I think

ROB: really? technicolor?

CUSTOMER 3: I think so...

CUSTOMER 4: whatever...

ROB: with an i ?

CUSTOMER 3: I think so... I think it's an i...

CUSTOMER 4: yeah, it's in my email address so that's [laughs] why I think...

ROB: it's your email address?

CUSTOMER 4: yes

ROB: one word?

CUSTOMER 4: yeah

ROB: and the word is technicolor... now it looks right, of course, with an i...

CUSTOMER 3: [laughs]

ROB: I wasn't so sure

CUSTOMER 5: [laughs]

ROB: ok... here's your receipt

CUSTOMER 4: thanks

ROB: you're welcome

CUSTOMER 4: here's your dollar

ROB: thank you... um... there you are

CUSTOMER 4: beautiful

ROB: did you get your dollar's worth?

CUSTOMER 4: yes

ROB: ok

CUSTOMER 4: definitely

ROB: good... you had a great experience?

CUSTOMER 4: [laughs]

ROB: all right... Casey, what are you thinking about?

CUSTOMER 5: I think I'm gonna do, um, better

ROB: better?

CUSTOMER 5: yes

ROB: nice word... um... ok and what is it gonna look like?

CUSTOMER 5: um... printed

ROB: printed on the computer?

CUSTOMER 5: no printed

ROB: printed, hand...

CUSTOMER 5: ...hand printed

ROB: hand printed... um... pen or marker?

CUSTOMER 5: um... pen

ROB: pen... ok... better... all right, good... uh, vertical? horizontal? somewhere on the page?

CUSTOMER 5: um vertical... just across the middle

ROB: vertical, across the middle, like this? like here?

CUSTOMER 5: uh-huh

ROB: ok... initial cap?

CUSTOMER 5: no

ROB: all lowercase... small? or large?

CUSTOMER 5: large

ROB: large, printed in the middle... interesting... ok let's see

CUSTOMER 3: wow

CUSTOMER 4: I know... that was really weird

ROB: about like that?

CUSTOMER 5: yeah

ROB: because we can always start over...

CUSTOMER 5: no

ROB: if it doesn't work, no? ok... part of... how's that?

CUSTOMER 5: I like it

ROB: I like that... see, part of my thing is I'm not, you know, really a professional. I'm really an amateur... and so, um, you know there's a lot of room to... to grow... ok, next... what are you thinking about?

CUSTOMER 3: um... I want you to surprise me with a word

ROB: ok

CUSTOMER 3: um, but I want to give you a direction

ROB: ok

CUSTOMER 3: I want the word to be spunky

ROB: spunky?

CUSTOMER 3: yeah I want it to be a spunky word... um, and I want you to write it in Sharpie as large as you can

ROB: Sharpie as large as I can... a spunky word...

CUSTOMER 3: ...um, in print

ROB: print...

CUSTOMER 3: ...um, and I want you decide on the capitals or non-capitals, and I want you not, not, not show me the word

ROB: you don't want to see it?

CUSTOMER 3: I don't want to see it, so I'm gonna close my eyes

ROB: all right... and I'm gonna write it large

CUSTOMER 3: as big as you can fit on the paper

ROB: all right

CUSTOMER 3: um, and then I want you to give it to me, uh, folded in half

ROB: so that you can't see it? ...so... and then...

CUSTOMER 3: ...so I can't see it

ROB: I'll put it into a folder

CUSTOMER 3: no I don't want a folder... I don't want any packaging

ROB: no packaging

CUSTOMER 3: yeah

ROB: ok... I'm ready

CUSTOMER 3: all right... actually, if you could just fold it as many times as you can in half

ROB: ok

CUSTOMER 3: that would be... be ideal

ROB: keep folding it?

CUSTOMER 3: yeah, I think seven is the… is that the…

CUSTOMER 4: yeah, that's the max

CUSTOMER 3: …the maximum, right? ok… so seven times, I want it folded seven times

ROB: why seven times?

CUSTOMER 3: that's just as many times you can fold any size paper

ROB: really?

CUSTOMER 3: I want it… after you fold it all up…

ROB: yeah?…

CUSTOMER 3: …stamped on, on one side, and signed on the other, as best you can

ROB: beautiful

CUSTOMER 3: I mean your whole stamp probably won't fit, maybe it will

ROB: well I'm… I got it folded now to a point where it will, but I could fold it once more

CUSTOMER 3: how many times did you fold it?

ROB: four

CUSTOMER 3: oh, you gotta keep folding

CUSTOMER 4: [laughs]

ROB: ok, seven is right… it's accurate, I think

CUSTOMER 3: yeah?

ROB: well, I... I don't even think I'm gonna make it. I mean seven is...

CUSTOMER 3: not even seven?

ROB: ...pushing it... seven's gonna be pushing it

CUSTOMER 3: I mean, as many as you can

ROB: this is six... I think this is...

CUSTOMER 3: is that it?

ROB: yeah

CUSTOMER 3: all right

ROB: that's it

CUSTOMER 3: I think seven is without atmosphere

ROB: oh, this works out really well... ok...

CUSTOMER 3: ok... thank you very much

ROB: you're welcome

CUSTOMER 3: oh that looks great like that

ROB: beautiful... I don't know if you ever want to open it

CUSTOMER 3: yeah I know... maybe I won't

ROB: that's very nice

CUSTOMER 3: I'm gonna go recycle it now

ROB: but you do need a receipt

CUSTOMER 3: I do

ROB: ...and, uh, you don't want any other packaging?

CUSTOMER 3: no please... thank you very much

ROB: great and the store is open for the whole month of May so if you...

CUSTOMER 3: ...Tuesday through Thursday every day right?

ROB: tell your friends...

CUSTOMER 3: ...to swing by

ROB: swing by

CUSTOMER 3: cool

ROB: you need a business card... there you go... and that's it... I'm gonna turn this off... and we did very, very well

Customer 6

ROB: ok... are we going?

CUSTOMER 6: yes

ROB: we should be... are you moving? are you frozen?

CUSTOMER 6: um

ROB: there you are?

CUSTOMER 6: here I am

ROB: yeah, no, we're good... ok... so, um, what can I do for you, what would you like?

CUSTOMER 6: um, well let's see, I guess... uh... um I had a word, and I, I don't remember what it was... how 'bout unscripted?

ROB: unscripted... great... now, wait... the printer is available if you're interested, um, and handwritten is...

CUSTOMER 6: I think, let's do handwritten

ROB: yep

CUSTOMER 6: yeah

ROB: I love that everybody's going for handwritten these days... ok... the word unscripted... very nice... um, marker or pen?

CUSTOMER 6: what do you... what do you suggest?

ROB: um, surprisingly, I think things have been coming out very nice with the marker

CUSTOMER 6: ok let's try it with the marker

ROB: marker... and, um, cursive or print?

CUSTOMER 6: um, print

ROB: excellent... large or small?

CUSTOMER 6: uh, let's do small

ROB: ok, so, small unscripted... why small?... any thoughts?

CUSTOMER 6: well I think I had initially been imagining it as fairly large and I thought I should... I... I... I... I wanted to contradict that impulse

ROB: ah, that's interesting

CUSTOMER 6: yeah

ROB: ah, ok, good and what about placement?

CUSTOMER 6: um, how 'bout sort of over toward the... the right side of it

ROB: on a landscape?

CUSTOMER 6: yeah, landscape, yeah

ROB: ok, um, and uh let's see, so we have print, we have fairly small, um, initial cap? no initial cap? any caps?

CUSTOMER 6: no, no caps

ROB: no caps then

CUSTOMER 6: well, um, maybe, maybe the... the... the c could be a cap

ROB: c a cap, that's nice, I like that... all right, so, I think I need about, um, [long pause] wow, that looks really strange. Is that spelled right?

CUSTOMER 6: yeah, I think so... it's upside down so

ROB: I think... I think it is

CUSTOMER 6: yeah

ROB: ok

CUSTOMER 6: yeah, that's... that's... that is nice

ROB: that's... uh... that's what you had in mind, huh?

CUSTOMER 6: yeah

ROB: terrific, uh, ok, stamp is good?

CUSTOMER 6: stamp is good

ROB: maybe, um, are you going back... when are you going back to Chicago?

CUSTOMER 6: uh, tomorrow

ROB: maybe we should do a free one for Judith?

CUSTOMER 6: that would be wonderful, yeah

ROB: terrific, ok... um... envelope or folder?... so far this project is happening totally different than I imagined

CUSTOMER 6: really? how so? what are the nature...

ROB: it hasn't happened, um, I like what's happening without me [unintelligible] anything...

CUSTOMER 6: ...right

ROB: ...directing anything

CUSTOMER 6: and this is day two? is that right?

ROB: day two, yeah

CUSTOMER 6: ok

ROB: yeah, yeah

CUSTOMER 6: so I imagine, uh, things will change as it... as it goes along

ROB: I guess you're right, yeah, I guess so... all right, so we got one word

CUSTOMER 6: have you done this sort of long-term project like this before at all?

ROB: never

CUSTOMER 6: yeah

ROB: never

CUSTOMER 6: it's really...

ROB: ...nothing...

CUSTOMER 6: yeah

ROB: ...durational

CUSTOMER 6: yeah... so wha-wha-wha-what was the impetus?

ROB: ...to be like totally public, um, so that was... that was part of it and the… and the other part of it was, really, what would be a logical step to, uh, my interest in poetry and consumerism… I wanted to enact it…

CUSTOMER 6: mm-hmm, mm-hmm

ROB: so that's the more real reason… than I woke up one morning…

CUSTOMER 6: well it's interesting because I mean the… the… the… they're a dollar each is that the…

ROB: yeah

CUSTOMER 6: so it's funny in that it… it's sort of… it seems to me at least to be kinda there… there… there… it's now we are making it into this conversation a little

ROB: ok

CUSTOMER 6: there it… it… there's a way in which it sort of oscillates between commodified because it's so… it… it… I'm… it'd be one thing if you were charging, say, you know 30 or 150 bucks or whatever

ROB: right

CUSTOMER 6: because it's… it's [inaudible]… it's… it's ac… there's almost a gift element to it

ROB: right

CUSTOMER 6: I like that

ROB: right, right, right, right… well it's the same… that's very interesting… 'cause for me that's the same idea that we have when we appropriate language

CUSTOMER 6: mm-hmm

ROB: appropriate it… it… it… it… it's not …there's a real, uh, exchange happening… ah let me put it more specifically, it's not about... I think when we appropriate language, it's not that you're... it's not that you're revivifying...

CUSTOMER 6: mm-hmm

ROB: ...you're more like drawing attention to its bankruptcy

CUSTOMER 6: mm-hmm, mm-hmm

ROB: so I think I'm doing that here in a certain way... I'm not trying to make money

CUSTOMER 6: yeah

ROB: I'm just trying to highlight the act...

CUSTOMER 6: right

ROB: ...of making money

CUSTOMER 6: right, mm-hmm

ROB: I'm not actually... yeah you're right... I'm not actually... I'm losing money... everyday I'm here, I'm losing money

CUSTOMER 6: yeah [laughs]... so... so, actually, you're really enacting capitalism in that way too

ROB: that's right yeah, yeah, and I'm never gonna, I'm al... I'm sure I'm going to spend more on supplies...

CUSTOMER 6: uh-huh

ROB: ...than I'm actually gonna...

CUSTOMER 6: uh-huh

ROB: ...gross... uh, yeah, yeah, so there is that too...

CUSTOMER 6: yeah, yeah, yeah

ROB: yeah, all right, so what would we do for, now, Judith? ... doesn't have to be one word...

CUSTOMER 6: ok

ROB: since it's a gift, you know, she could... yeah, so what should we do for Judith? we have to...

CUSTOMER 6: um... I, uh, off the books... something along those lines...

ROB: off the books?

CUSTOMER 6: yeah

ROB: that's good

Customer 7

CUSTOMER 7: Where's the video?

ROB: coming

CUSTOMER 7: oh, is it so you record your...

ROB: um, right so I'm... there we go

CUSTOMER 7: it gets... it gets both of us

ROB: well not actually

CUSTOMER 7: are you?... it's...

ROB: we don't really need me

CUSTOMER 7: oh, ok

ROB: it's... it's already seen enough of me... um, ok, so what words... that's what this is all about, it's all about whether, um, you want to pick a word or letter... whether you want me to pick it, whether you want us to do it collectively, uh, whether we're going to use something that's already been [inaudible]...

CUSTOMER 7: I'd be curious in either you picking it or you coming up with a few suggestions

ROB: oh, ok, uh-huh, all right

CUSTOMER 7: and then I choose from among them

ROB: among the suggestions?

CUSTOMER 7: yeah, yeah

ROB: terrific... all right, good, um, I would, well, since you are a critic and scholar I think maybe a word that is central to your thinking about some of the things you're writing about...

CUSTOMER 7: hmm

ROB: ...might be interesting

CUSTOMER 7: hmm

ROB: ...singular

CUSTOMER 7: now obviously the word that is, uh, most central to what I'm writing about is "constraint" right?... have I... have I told you?... I don't know if you remember my dissertation project I'm doing with, uh, Wayne... it's, uh, I'm... I'm writing about constraint-based writing

ROB: right

CUSTOMER 7: ...broadly defined, and doing it as a constraint-based exercise

ROB: right

CUSTOMER 7: however I think at this point the people that know I'm doing this project so associate me with this word or that if there's any piece of writing or art that's in some sense possibly constraint-based, they'll point it out to me and I actually get kind of sick of the word

ROB: right

CUSTOMER 7: I don't know if you have similar feelings vis-a-vis like the word "conceptual"

ROB: right, right

CUSTOMER 7: …for example

ROB: yeah, absolutely… yeah, yeah

CUSTOMER 7: so…

ROB: it's a love-hate relationship

CUSTOMER 7: yeah, yeah, I mean obviously I really like works that fall into this rubric

ROB: right

CUSTOMER 7: you know it's… and… it's, you know, as a way of working

ROB: right

CUSTOMER 7: but… and that would be the most logical word to choose…

ROB: right

CUSTOMER 7: related to what I do but, actually, it would be the one I would least… I'd be least interested…

ROB: right

CUSTOMER 7: … in…

ROB: …in living with…

CUSTOMER 7: in… yes, exactly [laughter]… exactly… and purchasing

ROB: right

CUSTOMER 7: I feel like I maybe, I've already...

ROB: right

CUSTOMER 7: ...bought it

ROB: right, uh...

CUSTOMER 7: I wonder if there's a word...

ROB: unless it was made in such a way... see, that's the other part of our conversation... is gonna be how it's made... it could be made in such a way that would ex... somehow exemplify or represent your ambivalence

CUSTOMER 7: hmm

ROB: ...uh, as an example or it could... or it could be, uh, yeah... I like constraint-based as [inaudible] one word

CUSTOMER 7: yeah as the hyphenated... though that's, uh, that to me always... 'cause I say that a lot in writing about constraint-based writing

ROB: right

CUSTOMER 7: but it... it's always kind of clumsy and awk...

ROB: ...right

CUSTOMER 7: you know 'cause it's... it's got that... that hyphen

ROB: yeah yeah

CUSTOMER 7: but we can do... yeah

ROB: I mean just as something to think about, you know, I mean, um, those are some thoughts... constraint...

CUSTOMER 7: do you... do you normally just write them on the piece of paper?... do you...

ROB: well we have a couple of choices, right, we right 'em on a piece of paper... you can decide... you have your choice between a Sharpie and a pen, cursive and print, also there's a printer, um, so it could be computer generated

CUSTOMER 7: ok

ROB: uh, it could be landscape or...

CUSTOMER 7: or p... ok

ROB: cool... it could be, uh, all caps, no caps, and those are basically the decisions [inaudible], um, but we're still on the word

CUSTOMER 7: yeah, yeah, yeah

ROB: it's complicated

CUSTOMER 7: well I was thinking given the options what are the... is there a way of doing... is there a way of picking an option that's some way constraint based?... perhaps not... not in terms of the choice of the word but how it's written, represented or...

ROB: something about how it's written that's constrained?

CUSTOMER 7: yeah, but that might be a little too involved for...

ROB: um, it could, uh, go off the page so that it was no longer constrained... the word constraint that...

CUSTOMER 7: maybe

ROB: maybe didn't quite fit

CUSTOMER 7: maybe constraint with like the dash and then the based... which we talked about, but gets lopped off or...

ROB: the based?

CUSTOMER 7: well, based... the word based

ROB: the word based starts... we start the word based and it goes off the end of the page…

CUSTOMER 7: or…

ROB: yeah…

CUSTOMER 7: you do constraint with a dash and the dash alone indicates that there's…

ROB: yeah…

CUSTOMER 7: …another half to the compound or something

ROB: yeah, yeah, yeah, maybe part of a b

CUSTOMER 7: yeah some… something like that

ROB: get the… oh, that could be interesting… ok, good, so then it sounds like, um, it should be pretty big… you think, or no?

CUSTOMER 7: yeah I don't have a…

ROB: …or it doesn't go off

CUSTOMER 7: … vision… yeah, I… I guess… so that it doesn't look like it's deliberately off the…

ROB: or, or it could just be like that much text and go off the end, or it could be really big and then run out of space…

CUSTOMER 7: I had a… when I thought of that I pictured it coming, you know, just… just being like a, you know, normal size font or lettering

ROB: mm-hmm, mm-hmm…

CUSTOMER 7: but then that would look like a very calculated…

ROB: mm-hmm

CUSTOMER 7: …decision as opposed to if it was massive and it just ran out of space

ROB: right, right

CUSTOMER 7: that might be more interesting in terms of thinking about the page as a limit

ROB: mm-hmm

CUSTOMER 7: or boundary…

ROB: mm-hmm

CUSTOMER 7: …of some sort

ROB: mm-hmm

CUSTOMER 7: …that you know restricts the word so that…

ROB: right

CUSTOMER 7: although I don't know how it would look al… although maybe that would be the way to do it with the Sharpie

ROB: right

CUSTOMER 7: that would cause the, you know, the…

ROB: …I can see that with a Sharpie and then, uh, caps or no caps you think?

CUSTOMER 7: I don't know

ROB: print or… print or cursive that will probably answer the first question

CUSTOMER 7: pr… print I think

ROB: print, I, ok let's try it… let's try it all caps

CUSTOMER 7: sure

ROB: all caps sounds good?

CUSTOMER 7: yeah… yep…

ROB: let's see what that would look like middle of the page more or less

CUSTOMER 7: ok… that's perfect… I like that

ROB: yeah, what do you think?

CUSTOMER 7: yeah

ROB: cool

CUSTOMER 7: yeah I… I think that worked

ROB: good… it's the most complex… the most complex word of the store… it's challenging to the entrepreneur… ok, now would you like it, uh, stamped on the back?

CUSTOMER 7: sure I mean is that the… is that the…

ROB: …typically I stamp it on the back and sign…

CUSTOMER 7: is your computer… is it still getting us?

ROB: yeah

CUSTOMER 7: even if the screen is off?

ROB: it does… it does… in fact… in fact, we even looked up words… we went online and did the dictionary…

CUSTOMER 7: and the…

ROB: …and… and…

CUSTOMER 7: camera still…

ROB: …and it was still going and it's like you're looking really closely at the screen… it's really good…

Customer 8

ROB: ok... good you came in with a word, excellent, all right

CUSTOMER 8: it is nachleben

ROB: nachleben... beautiful, um, now we have a choice of... such a beautiful word, what does it mean?

CUSTOMER 8: "afterlife"... it's... um, ah, I know it from Aby Warburg, ah, who used it in talking about his [inaudible] and other... other things... it was an idea [inaudible] "afterlife" and, uh, um, it has... it has another sense too but... but literally...

ROB: mm-hmm

CUSTOMER 8: uh... etymologically...

ROB: mm-hmm

CUSTOMER 8: ...it's "afterlife"

ROB: beautiful word... now we have our choices of... I could write it with a pen... I could write it with a Sharpie... or we could do it on the computer

CUSTOMER 8: uh, with a pen I think

ROB: a pen... ok, um, vertical or horizontal?

CUSTOMER 8: uh, I think vertical like that

ROB: vertical like this?... some other questions that are interesting... we have to think about... um, script or print?

CUSTOMER 8: um... script

ROB: script would echo a certain eloquence, I think, of the word

CUSTOMER 8: yeah, yeah

ROB: print would seem a little childish maybe with this word

CUSTOMER 8: yeah

ROB: yeah... all right... script it is... initial cap?

CUSTOMER 8: ah... no

ROB: beautiful... all right... placement? middle of the page? top? bottom? left? right?

CUSTOMER 8: just about the middle

ROB: just about the middle, so looking sort of... in here?

CUSTOMER 8: mm-hmm

ROB: oh wait... wait... vertical right? ok, very good... all right now spelling, ok?

CUSTOMER 8: no, this is, um, n-a-c-h

ROB: n-a-c-h

CUSTOMER 8: l-e-b-e-n

ROB: l-e-v-e ?

CUSTOMER 8: nah... *b*... *b*...

ROB: l-e-b

CUSTOMER 8: nachleben

ROB: nachleben

CUSTOMER 8: right... spring-life

ROB: or ever-life

CUSTOMER 8: right, right, right, the good life [laughs]

ROB: right, of course, uh [inaudible] ok... good... so we're lower case and scripted and we're sort of right around here... I think not...

not real big... medium size... normal size

CUSTOMER 8: um, yeah, not real big but not... I would say kind of to fit the page

ROB: to fit the page right... all right, very good... good?

CUSTOMER 8: uh-huh

ROB: typically I put a stamp on the back

CUSTOMER 8: ah-ha

ROB: is that good?

CUSTOMER 8: yeah, yeah, yeah...

ROB: you know what's funny about this project for me... I was talking to somebody that it's not very original... in fact, in the "Phantom Tollbooth", I think, in the kid's story, there's a word shop

CUSTOMER 8: oh [inaudible]

ROB: yeah... yeah, but they're edible... they're edible

CUSTOMER 8: ah

DAY 3

Ledger

Left apartment at 11:00 on bicycle. Arrived at Rob's Word Shop at 11:05 AM and quickly set up shop. I had no customers today, but I did have 2 requests for mail orders and 1 hand-delivery. Left the shop at 2:10 PM, dropped off hand-delivery, and bicycled home. Arrived at my apartment around 2:18 PM.

>   *Hand Delivery Customer: the letter S*
>
>   *Mail Order Customer 1: On errands of life, these letters speed to death.*
>
>   *Mail Order Customer 2: feldspar and gones*

Total sales: $11.50 (payment pending).

DAY 4

Ledger

Left apartment at 10:45 on foot (rain). Arrived at Rob's Word Shop at 10:55. Set up shop between 11:00-11:15.

First customer, Customer 9, arrived around 11:45 and purchased 1 word and 3 letters for $2.50. 1 letter was given gratis because the printer was not printing properly. This was the first customer to request a computer printed document. The word was mouth—there was an additional e at the end and an n underneath. Also, the letters o and n were hand-written over the ut of mouth.

Customer 10 arrived around 12:30 and purchased 1 word: footprint. This word was generated by the customer's initial word, wince. After some research on the word wince we learned that "wince footprint" is the name of a software program. We decided that the 2 words were very nice together and so I wrote in marker wince footprint. I only charged $1 for 1 word because the first word was primarily a generator for the 2nd word.

Customer 11, the owner of the storefront, ordered the word Poetry for $1.

I bought a turkey sandwich at the Celebrate café, run by the Lower East Side Girls Club, and left the profits of the day for a tip. I left at 2:15 and walked back to my apartment. I arrived there at 2:28 PM.

Total sales: $4.50

Customer 9

ROB: all right now, let's hope this is working... yeah, all right good... ok, good, so just finishing here... and with Suzanne... and just so we get a sense... in case we never see it again so this is what we ended up with which is initially mouth but which also has an extra e and an extra n at the bottom and an o and an n handwritten on top... ok? good? um... all right...

CUSTOMER 9: well thank you very much

ROB: did you have a satisfactory transaction?

CUSTOMER 9: this was, um, this was the most enjoyable shopping pleasure... it was like buying a new hat

ROB: I'm so happy

CUSTOMER 9: do you have change for a ten dollars?

ROB: well that's a tough one because you're my first customer today

CUSTOMER 9: [inaudible] say that all the time?

ROB: yes, exactly, let me see if I can make some change from the uh...

CUSTOMER 9: people?

ROB: people

CUSTOMER 9: no, I thought of it as I left the house my, uh, my coin jar [pause]... Rob, you are going to have so much dead air time? ...it's very strange, I've never done Skype so looking at myself talking is very odd

ROB: [laughs] maybe you... maybe...

CUSTOMER 9: actually I think I like myself in this [inaudible]...

not like that where I have my eyes open… it's all right, but when it's like…

ROB: oh, I just made a mistake, now wait a minute… you're… do you… I kinda didn't do this right

CUSTOMER 9: I thought you were gonna get change from her?

ROB: I did but I didn't get enough… do you have anything other than a ten dollars?

CUSTOMER 9: um… I've thirty-seven cents

ROB: [laughs]

CUSTOMER 9: and, uh, [inaudible] when one changes one's pants

ROB: otherwise I'm gonna get two fives

CUSTOMER 9: I always think secretly at the bottom [inaudible]

ROB: …that you have… let me get more change [inaudible]

CUSTOMER 9: oh wow, I have two cameras

ROB: ok, we're in business, at every opportunity, um, the uh…

CUSTOMER 9: yeah?

ROB: …the lack of professionalism of my store becomes, uh, transparent

CUSTOMER 9: well the first day you were five minutes late

ROB: for instance… no, no, second day… yeah, first day I was fifteen minutes early… yeah… yeah

CUSTOMER 9: thank you very much

ROB: you're so welcome… it's a pleasure doing business with you… come back, I'm here all month

CUSTOMER 9: oh it's all month

ROB: it's all month

CUSTOMER 9: ah…

ROB: …and at the end, this conversation will be, um, somehow made into a book… all of the conversations

CUSTOMER 9: without all this dead time?

ROB: well that won't be part of it, but I don't know what's going to happen with the, uh, videos

CUSTOMER 9: uh huh

ROB: maybe something

CUSTOMER 9: yeah

ROB: probably something

CUSTOMER 9: who knows how they might be scrambled or refastened

ROB: exactly

CUSTOMER 9: or not used at all

ROB: right

CUSTOMER 9: well thank you

ROB: you're so welcome, all right

CUSTOMER 9: oh, how much would you charge for the book based on Rob's Word Shop prices?

Customer 10

ROB: so…

CUSTOMER 10: I thought those were customers for the store

ROB: right… no, unfortunately… now typically the way this has worked is that people decide whether they want their word handwritten or printed, whether they've already come in with a word or want to decide on a word or words or letter with me, or in the room, or online, or, uh all those kinds of choices… um… they could be printed with the printer which actually is not behaving very well…

CUSTOMER 10: maybe I'll take the, uh, handwritten

ROB: …they could be handwritten, yeah

CUSTOMER 10: and how much are they?

ROB: words are one dollar and letters are fifty cents… most people have chosen to take an individual word although some people have taken clusters of words and even a sentence or two, but I would say for the most part, uh, it has been, um, a word… and then you have the choice of… then there's a lot of choices and, ah, and you can make those choices or you can have me make them, such as, uh, would you like a marker or a pen?… those are the two choices… cursive or print?… size? placement? all that

CUSTOMER 10: oh, ok, on an 8½" by 11" piece…

ROB: …yeah

CUSTOMER 10: ok?

ROB: or it could be a scrap of paper… I mean it could be, you know…

CUSTOMER 10: yeah, ok, I'll just take that 8½" by 11"…

ROB: all right

CUSTOMER 10: and I'll have the large marker

ROB: all right

CUSTOMER 10: and print, non-cursive style

ROB: non-cursive

CUSTOMER 10: no, I'm sorry... I'm sorry, cursive style

ROB: cursive style, all right, and horizontal or vertical?

CUSTOMER 10: vertical

ROB: ok, all right, so...

CUSTOMER 10: top...

ROB: now all we need...

CUSTOMER 10: ...top of the page

ROB: top of the...

CUSTOMER 10: ...somewhere... somewhere on the top third of the page

ROB: top... top center

CUSTOMER 10: uh, yeah, center... there you go [inaudible]

ROB: all right

CUSTOMER 10: all right... I do have a word but I'd like... I don't want to buy that word unless it's absolutely necessary... what I'd like to do is, uh, contribute the word... throw out the word... and have it generate another word or two

ROB: mm-hmm

CUSTOMER 10: ...that something could precede this word or be subsequent to the word or both

ROB: sounds very interesting… ok

CUSTOMER 10: so… and I… and you know you're generating processes would be good

ROB: ok… [off] see you later…

CUSTOMER 10: they got burgers here?

ROB: no

CUSTOMER 10: is the food any good? ok, ok…

ROB: I mean there's… there's some… they might have a good soup, like they had gumbo yesterday

CUSTOMER 10: I'll run down to the Italian place…

ROB: …yeah… they have gumbo

CUSTOMER 10: …see if it's open…

ROB: um… the… Pulino?

CUSTOMER 10: yeah

ROB: I'm curious about that place

CUSTOMER 10: it's not bad

ROB: all right

CUSTOMER 10: yeah… the word is wince

ROB: wince?

CUSTOMER 10: w-i-n-c-e

ROB: mm-hmm

CUSTOMER 10: and I guess that could be a noun or a verb couldn't it? is there a wince?

ROB: I don't know of it as a noun

CUSTOMER 10: yeah… is it just a verb?

ROB: I think it might just be a verb… uh-huh… ok, wince…

CUSTOMER 10: maybe, he didn't have, like, a strange wince or painful wince?

ROB: uh, maybe so

CUSTOMER 10: I don't know

ROB: yeah

CUSTOMER 10: I'm not sure

ROB: no, no, that sounds good… that sounds, uh… that sounds believable, um, I like hither

CUSTOMER 10: hither?

ROB: mm-hmm

CUSTOMER 10: wince and hither… hither?

ROB: umm…

CUSTOMER 10: hither… that sounds a little to me… that's… a, uh, a little historic… or, uh, archaic

ROB: mm-hmm, mm-hmm… more archaic than wince?

CUSTOMER 10: yeah

ROB: uh-huh

CUSTOMER 10: yeah wince was kind of a, uh, for me it has a sense of cultural… contemporary… cultural criticism

ROB: mm-hmm

CUSTOMER 10: …about it… yeah, wince hither… hither wince…

hither wince... have a nice sound to them

ROB: mm-hmm, mm-hmm, that's all right

CUSTOMER 10: hither wince

ROB: hither wince

CUSTOMER 10: or just hither on its own... letting wince generate that word hither

ROB: mm-hmm

CUSTOMER 10: wow that's quite a stretch actually

ROB: mm-hmm

CUSTOMER 10: it's an interesting stretch though

ROB: mm-hmm

CUSTOMER 10: no doubt

ROB: well let's keep that one in the air and keep thinking

CUSTOMER 10: all right

ROB: um... wince... um... um...

CUSTOMER 10: you ever Google... you ever use, um, online...

ROB: yeah, um...

CUSTOMER 10: ...sources?

ROB: aids and tools... well, we used a dictionary to check a spelling and we were very happy to see that the video was still working

CUSTOMER 10: hmm...

ROB: and as we look at the screen we, uh, intently... to get the correct spelling... that was reflected in the video

CUSTOMER 10: mmm...

ROB: which was very nice

CUSTOMER 10: yeah

ROB: the intensity of our, um, I think that's a very...

CUSTOMER 10: [inaudible]

ROB: what would happen?... but I think this is a very interesting idea... let's see if we go to wince... wince... wince 6.0?

Customer 11

ROB: here we go... all right, so we're talking about the word poetry, um, we have a few things to decide... first of all, if we want it printed on a printer, or done with a pen, or a Sharpie... those are our choices

CUSTOMER 11: Sharpie please

ROB: Sharpie... very good, uh, horizontal or vertical?

CUSTOMER 11: um, horizontal

ROB: and script or print?

CUSTOMER 11: print

ROB: interesting... why print? any... any feelings?

CUSTOMER 11: I'm scared of your cursive

ROB: my cursive... scared of my cursive?

CUSTOMER 11: yeah I mean... you know... I mean... I'm admiring your outfit which seems totally appropriate... funereal, you know, as if this were the death of the word by selling it... which is always what I've thought about the poem... it's that one, uh, economic form that... that stands up to the Goliath of Capitalism

ROB: that's it

CUSTOMER 11: the poetic form, the poem can't be, uh, bought and yet I'm gonna buy poetry now for a buck so I'm feeling good... but... I prefer if you just printed it out

ROB: keep the subjectivity out of it a little bit...

CUSTOMER 11: a little bit...

ROB: ...you don't know what you're gonna get

CUSTOMER 11: ...I mean you're a pretty subjective kinda guy

ROB: all right... so we're gonna have print... we're gonna have, uh, caps or initial cap?

CUSTOMER 11: could you do, uh, a large cap and the others in small caps?

ROB: initial cap and then small... you got it

CUSTOMER 11: yeah

ROB: sounds very good... large?... writ large in general? medium?

CUSTOMER 11: could I leave that up to you?

ROB: of course

CUSTOMER 11: I'm gonna leave that one up to you

ROB: and then the other thing is whether you wanna leave placement up to me or whether you want it at the top, middle, bottom...?

CUSTOMER 11: I would like to leave placement up to you

ROB: beautiful

CUSTOMER 11: do you sign these by the way?

ROB: I do… they get stamped and signed

CUSTOMER 11: ok, great

ROB: …on the back, unless you want it on the front?

CUSTOMER 11: I would like it on the front if you don't mind

ROB: you got it… all right, so there's our P

CUSTOMER 11: nice, it's a good one

ROB: there's our o and t

CUSTOMER 11: I'm, uh, pleased

ROB: it's not bad… ok?

DAY 5

Ledger

Left apartment at 10:53 on bicycle. Arrived at Rob's Word Shop at 11:00 sharp. Set up from 11:00-11:12. Organized ledger and receipts from 11:15-11:30. First customer arrived around 11:30. I was continually busy with 5 customers from 11:30 until closing at 2 PM. My assistant, Lawrence, was in the shop most of the day documenting several transactions.

Left the shop around 2 PM on bicycle, stopped for lunch with customer, arrived home around 3:40 PM.

    Customer 12: the small form
    Customer 13A: BEANS DEAR?
    Customer 13: S and S (this now makes "S" our most popular item)
    Customer 14: diarrahea z
    Customer 15: nizes and shape / An overall blend

Total sales: $12.50.

Customer 12

ROB: all right we're good... it's enough to keep me totally busy... ok, you got an idea?

CUSTOMER 12: well I want a... I thought we should talk about it

ROB: ok...

CUSTOMER 12: ...first

ROB: ...tell me what's on your mind

CUSTOMER 12: well... like... I wanted a couple of words

ROB: yeah

CUSTOMER 12: but... and I thought of a couple of words, but I don't know if I actually want them... so I thought maybe you had an idea

ROB: I... I could counsel as to whether or not you actually want those words or other words

CUSTOMER 12: a couple words and an article

ROB: and an article?

CUSTOMER 12: I was thinking... the small form

ROB: yeah

CUSTOMER 12: but I don't know if I really want those words

ROB: the small form?

CUSTOMER 12: yeah

ROB: oh, I think it's very good, the words are good and then you have to think about... if you decide to go with the small form which I think is interesting, then you have some choices to think about what it would look like… so maybe that would influence your decision on the small form

CUSTOMER 12: yeah

ROB: it's up to you whether you're committed to the small form

CUSTOMER 12: I think I am… it's like… it's one of the first things I thought of…

ROB: yeah, all right, good… so then you could think about whether you want that printed on the computer which, um, is there… or handwritten… and then you have two choices: one is a Sharpie and one is a pen… the small form is very interesting because it could be tiny… could be huge…

CUSTOMER 12: yeah

ROB: um… got a lot to play with

CUSTOMER 12: well I think I want it handwritten

ROB: handwritten all right… now we've gotta give a little bit of thought… while you're thinking about large and small the other thing is, um, horizontal or vertical… it's an issue

CUSTOMER 12: it's a big [inaudible]… I think vertical

ROB: beautiful

CUSTOMER 12: and maybe if you wrote it in pen and you made it sort of like full… the, like, width…

ROB: beautiful, so just with pen going cro… all the way, almost like off the page… the whole length of the…

CUSTOMER 12: …yeah but it doesn't need to necessarily be like equally spaced, but you're… you want to write where you're trying to get to the end but maybe doesn't even get there

ROB: all right I might run out

CUSTOMER 12: or you might like leave a big gap

ROB: all right beautiful, um, is this gonna be cursive or print?

CUSTOMER 12: yeah, cursive

ROB: cursive great and, um, all lowercase or initial cap?

CUSTOMER 12: I think... I think the... the... should be... the t should be capitalized...

ROB: capital T

CUSTOMER 12: ...and the rest lowercase?

ROB: and everything else is lowercase... good... all right so let's see... we're going to kinda go off the page... we're cursive... the small form... ok let's see now... the... small...

CUSTOMER 12: yeah...

ROB: can I run off?

CUSTOMER 12: yeah like the... maybe the m is cut off so you can...

ROB: beautiful

CUSTOMER 12: yeah

ROB: small form

CUSTOMER 12: yeah

ROB: uh, now, but I also made a mistake because these are also initial cap... you like that or should we do another one?

CUSTOMER 12: yeah I like that

ROB: you like that... all right, very good... um, stamp on the front or back or not at all?

CUSTOMER 12: yeah on the front maybe... wherever... wherever it lands

ROB: how's that?

CUSTOMER 12: very nice

ROB: thing of beauty... very nice... all right, good, now, um, we're good?

CUSTOMER 12: mm-hmm

ROB: beautiful let me...

CUSTOMER 12: ...settle up?

ROB: ...get you a receipt... settle up... now would you like this in a folder or in an envelope?

CUSTOMER 12: um...

ROB: it comes free of charge

CUSTOMER 12: yeah, I'll take a folder

ROB: you got it... ok, so we've got three words at three dollars... uh, three words I don't think any of these words have been used by the way... I don't even think *the* has been used yet so that's exciting... three words and they are: the... small... form... love it, thank you very much... exact change is much appreciated

CUSTOMER 12: thank you

ROB: thank you... very nice... ok, let's move on to our next transaction

Customers 13 and 13A

ROB: it's up to you... most people are videotaped... I... I don't know if I'm gonna use the video

CUSTOMER 13: all right, I'll do what most people do

ROB: I... yeah, that's the... that's, uh, that's the thing... um, I don't know what I'm gonna do with the videotape... there it is... but we'll see if I'm gonna do anything or not

CUSTOMER 13: that's a very official looking ledger

ROB: and look at my time card

CUSTOMER 13: oh yeah... that's good

ROB: yeah, that's one directly from Mr. Giffin

CUSTOMER 13: oh he got you that

ROB: yeah

CUSTOMER 13: good

ROB: well he's my records manager... I was complaining to him that I don't have much of a staff here, you know, there's no, uh, there's no one getting me coffee... there's a surprise... uh, it's really kind of, you know, he's doing a pretty ok job

CUSTOMER 13: considering that you're the CEO

ROB: you know I hired him to, uh, take care of these things

CUSTOMER 13: is he coming in today?

ROB: he is... see I thought those might be potential customers who I didn't know but it doesn't look like it, so I've had some...

CUSTOMER 13: ...you need a sign with color no one's gonna... nobody's eye is gonna be caught by this black and white sign

ROB: is that true?

CUSTOMER 13: yeah

ROB: because, um, Kim said the same thing

CUSTOMER 13: yeah I think so

ROB: I could get color makers

CUSTOMER 13: yeah, I think that's all you need… something… cause I think that…

ROB: some colored Sharpies

CUSTOMER 13: …that's kind of like the sign on a laundry mat, you know, or something

ROB: I'm kinda going for that

CUSTOMER 13: yeah but you need some customers

ROB: yeah and more street traffic

CUSTOMER 13: the laundry mat has a service that people need, so, you know, they're gonna kinda, you know, walk…

ROB: yeah exactly, ok, so… um… eee… uh, I… I think you probably have a sense of how this works… you can either have a word or you can have me [inaudible] a word or you can have a letter or a series of letters

CUSTOMER 13: mm-hmm

ROB: um, they can be printed on the computer, they can be… uh… uh… handwritten by me, and if they are handwritten by me there are two utensils that I use: a Sharpie or a black pen

CUSTOMER 13: mm-hmm

ROB: those are your only options and, uh, oh I found the paper… we can do all kinds of things so…

CUSTOMER 13: perfect

ROB: ...so first you have to decide if you want it handwritten and then we have to decide things like...

CUSTOMER 13: ...well what is your... what's the most popular option?

ROB: handwritten

CUSTOMER 13: handwritten?

ROB: yeah

CUSTOMER 13: with which... with which pen?

ROB: um handwritten with Sharpie... so far, just barely, lot of people go with the pen but, uh, but handwritten with Sharpie has been the most popular

CUSTOMER 13: what do you... do you have a best selling word or letter or anything?

ROB: no, in fact [inaudible]... in fact there have been no repeats

CUSTOMER 13: no repeats?

ROB: not at all

CUSTOMER 13: so if I... if I repeat something, then I can choose what becomes your bestselling word or letter?

ROB: yeah if you, in fact... if you had a word [inaudible] twice that would become the best selling word

CUSTOMER 13: so I can create this market

ROB: you could

CUSTOMER 13: all right

ROB: and there's also, right, if you buy a word somebody else could buy it too... I could tell people you have the best selling word

CUSTOMER 13: yeah, all right, I think I'm gonna go with that option, so these are the…

ROB: so…

CUSTOMER 13: so what has been sold so far… what are my options?

ROB: oh, everything's open… the stock…

CUSTOMER 13: …oh yeah, but I want to repeat something

ROB: oh you want to repeat something that already exists? I can't give you all of the words because, um, my documentation is somewhat incomplete…

CUSTOMER 13: hmm…

ROB: …from the first day but, uh, we have the word constraint b… we have: better, technicolor, tops, nachleben, off the books, poetry, and unscripted

CUSTOMER 13: none of these are really…

ROB: …jumping out at you?

CUSTOMER 13: …jumping out at me, yeah

ROB: uh, we have selfhood and escape, um, we have feldspar and gomes… the letter S… we have on errands of life these letters speed to death… uh…

CUSTOMER 13: let's think… the letter S is kind of attractive

ROB [OFF]: hey-ey-ey, look who's here!

CUSTOMER 13: oh man

ROB: you grew it out and shaved it off… looking beautiful

CUSTOMER 13A: hey, I wanna buy a couple of words

ROB: all right you have to get in line

CUSTOMER 13A: oh yeah?

ROB: it's not gonna be a long one... you wanna get a cup of coffee?

CUSTOMER 13A: no no... I'm just coming to hang out a little bit

ROB: how was your trip?

CUSTOMER 13A: ah it was nice... it was nice... a lot of fun

ROB: yeah... nothing extraordinary to tell us?

CUSTOMER 13A: ah, just another rage against... I was in Prague... just another European city

ROB: with beautiful bridges

CUSTOMER 13A: yeah, no, it was pretty... yeah, I'm tired [inaudible]

ROB: you're tired of traveling period?

CUSTOMER 13: tired of the world

CUSTOMER 13A: no we had a good time together

ROB: yeah, without the kids?

CUSTOMER 13A: yeah

ROB: very nice

CUSTOMER 13A: [to customer 13] yeah, so what are you buying?

CUSTOMER 13: I'm not sure yet... I'm trying to buy a word that will become the best selling word

CUSTOMER 13A: while you think about it, I'll grab one?

CUSTOMER 13: you already got it?... all right

CUSTOMER 13A: you think about it...

ROB: well if you're ready...

CUSTOMER 13A: I'm ready

ROB: all right

CUSTOMER 13: should I turn it toward [inaudible] so we can record him?

ROB: we're recording...

CUSTOMER 13A: what?

ROB: ...and everything is being recorded

CUSTOMER 13A: ok

Customer 14

CUSTOMER 14: there's no censorship of content of words?

ROB: absolutely not

CUSTOMER 14: and you know how to spell the words

ROB: well if I don't we look 'em up

CUSTOMER 14: ok... diarrhea

ROB: that's the word?... good one... um let's see and we're talking about the Sharpie or the pen?

CUSTOMER 14: um... maybe... maybe the Sharpie... it makes more of a... well... let's do a comparison... it seems like a bolder way, you know, I think there's two r's... r-r-h-e-a... r-h-e-a

ROB [OFF]: oh, hey... this is my records manager, Lawrence Giffin

CUSTOMER 14: hey what's up Lawrence?

ROB: this is Andy Lampert... Andy did some of the films at poetry project last week... that last Friday night thing, there were some films... filmmaker par excellence

CUSTOMER 14: yeah, it was fun... so where were we... so...

ROB [OFF]: ...you just missed Steve... he was here about...

LAWRENCE [OFF]: he was?... aw, that's too bad, I must have walked past him

ROB [OFF]: in fact, we're gonna have lunch right after at two o'clock if you're...

LAWRENCE [OFF]: I have to go back around then, but maybe... I'll... maybe I'll walk over with you

CUSTOMER 14: ...so maybe we'll go Sharpie on this?

ROB: ok

CUSTOMER 14: and, uh, and then, uh, after you're doing that I'm... um... I'm gonna buy a, uh, separate letter

ROB: mm-hmm beautiful... now we gotta think about whether we want it horizontal or vertical... landscape or more...

CUSTOMER 14: no I... I think landscape

ROB: um... we have to think about, um, any caps, initial cap, all caps, no caps

CUSTOMER 14: um... all caps... I think it's kinda... may... may... maybe like where just a litt... like down here a little bit

ROB: mm-hmm... business is jumping today gentlemen

CUSTOMER 14: maybe if you, if you, if you go from like right here with the d...

ROB: yeah, yeah

CUSTOMER 14: …end right about there

ROB: all right

CUSTOMER 14: …just left of center

ROB: yeah

CUSTOMER 14: yeah, I'd say that's good

ROB: that's about right?

ROB: yeah… beautiful… ok, we're gonna go kinda thick [inaudible]

CUSTOMER 14: yeah I would

ROB: all right here we go

CUSTOMER 14: and I would like to buy a, uh, a lowercase… ooh… ah lowercase? uh, I want to buy a z

ROB: mm-hmm

CUSTOMER 14: but, uh, like that bigger case… or cause it's not really…

ROB: I think, so, um, I cross my z… do you want a crossed z or not?

CUSTOMER 14: yeah, yeah, yeah, yeah

ROB: so here we go… we're gonna skip a space, same line, but we're gonna skip a little bit of a space… it could also be less sharp with… uh… and maybe it would be hugging more this… uh… uh right side

CUSTOMER 14: yeah

ROB: all right

CUSTOMER 14: ah, oh yeah… perfect!

ROB: beautiful

CUSTOMER 14: that's really good... that's really good!

ROB: all righty then... diarrhea z... would you like a stamp on the front or the back or not at all?

CUSTOMER 14: oh yeah I'd like a stamp... sure... uh... and the stamp can be anywhere

ROB: I usually end up with it in the corner but it could go anywhere... it's entirely up to you

CUSTOMER 14: down... up... right there, mmm, right there... oh couldn't be better

ROB: all right I'll date that and sign it... all right and then the only thing we have to do... a receipt and you can have a, uh, nice... you can... you can have a... uh...

CUSTOMER 14: ...can I have a protective envelope?... oh fantastic!

ROB: there you go... you got a protective envelope

CUSTOMER 14: cool

ROB: and my receipt pad's right here... just have to hook you up... hope you feel you had a successful transaction...

CUSTOMER 14: I absolutely did... this was... it wasn't on my mind...

ROB: this particular word you mean?

CUSTOMER 14: ...this particular word... but then when I... when I emptied my mind, it was! ...so that's pretty good

ROB: yeah that is very interesting... so we go... it's unusual but no one has ordered... oh, no one person has ordered a word... no... no one has ordered just one word and one letter... you're a first... that's, uh, people have had various combinations but not that one

CUSTOMER 14: you don't happen to have change do you?

ROB: I... I do have, well, I don't know if I have change for a twenty...

CUSTOMER 14: hmm... I don't have anything else unfortunately

ROB: well you just might have to uh...

CUSTOMER 14: ...get some change

ROB: ...drop by the shop some other time

CUSTOMER 14: I can IOU?

ROB: you can IO-me... see we can put some...

CUSTOMER 14: no, I can give you the fifty cents now and owe you a buck...

ROB: we'll take the fifty and then we'll see if we got change... I might

CUSTOMER 14: I don't want to blow your wad though for other purchasers

ROB: fifteen, sixteen, seventeen, eighteen... I got it! I got change!

CUSTOMER 14: oh, you really do

ROB: I really do... I can barely believe it, but I do... ok five, ten, fifteen, sixteen, seventeen, eighteen, nineteen dollars

CUSTOMER 14: ok, so there's twent dollars and there's fifty cents

ROB: thank you very much

CUSTOMER 14: thank you

ROB: you're welcome... did you get your receipt?

CUSTOMER 14: oh no... I'd like one, thank you very much

ROB: what did I do with it?

CUSTOMER 14: how much do you have to make before you declare this?

ROB: you mean in terms of, like, business?

CUSTOMER 14: yeah

ROB: ...and taxes?

CUSTOMER 14: yeah

ROB: um...

CUSTOMER 14: it's like $600 or something

ROB: I don't know... we [inaudible]... I think you got... did... did I give it to you?... that's very weird... take a look and see what happened to it... I could always make another one... oh, no, wait it's right here

CUSTOMER 14: oh, ok... thank you very much

ROB: thank you... I hope you had a very nice transaction

CUSTOMER 14: you're here again for another two weeks?

ROB: I'm here for two more weeks

CUSTOMER 14: ok, I'm gonna try...

ROB: ...take a card on your way out if you'd like

CUSTOMER 14: I will and I'd like to send, ah, some business your way from, ah, from Anthology... plus I might have a couple more words in me

ROB: you never know

CUSTOMER 14: yeah

ROB: especially with a word like the one you chose, you might have many more words

CUSTOMER 14: I hope so… loose words

Customer 15

ROB: ok you ready Andy?

CUSTOMER 15: yep

ROB: ok

CUSTOMER 15: all right, so I have a group of six words

ROB: six words

CUSTOMER 15: I'd like um…

ROB: …feeling, uh…

CUSTOMER 15: …frivolous today

ROB: frivolous… I was looking for the right word

CUSTOMER 15: I'm [inaudible] a rich day… um

ROB: ok, six words

CUSTOMER 15: I… they're underlined…

ROB: ok

CUSTOMER 15: in this… it's, uh, an erasure from this…

ROB: from an article "the origins of specificity in protein DNA recognition"… fantastic title, um, ok… so [unintelligible] those 3…

CUSTOMER 15: those 3…

ROB: ok, great, six altogether… beautiful do you want them to have that form?

CUSTOMER 15: I like the form and I like the cursive pen and I like capitalizing each word

ROB: form... cursive... pen... capitalize each form...

CUSTOMER 15: yeah

ROB: you got it

CUSTOMER 15: ...and so roughly fills the page

ROB: ok

CUSTOMER 15: use the whole thing

ROB: but you want it with a pen not a marker?...

CUSTOMER 15: yeah with a pen

ROB: great... vertical or horizontal

CUSTOMER 15: I guess what would you do?... I don't know...

ROB: well if you want to fill the page you might want to go vertical

CUSTOMER 15: ok

ROB: if you really want to fill the page, I would recommend going with the marker... depends on how...

CUSTOMER 15: how does the marker cursive look?

ROB: I think they come out very handsome

CUSTOMER 15: yeah, I like that

ROB: how can you lose?... ok, so these are... did we say cursive?

CUSTOMER 15: yeah cursive

ROB: but initial cap?

CUSTOMER 15: initial cap

ROB: all right... so... and we're going to try to take as much space as possible

CUSTOMER 15: yeah

ROB: ok so we got [inaudible] and shape [inaudible] skip [inaudible]

[recording cuts off]

DAY 6

Ledger

Left the apartment, walking, at 10:53 (rain), and arrived at Rob's Word Shop at 11:01. Set up shop from 11:05-11:30. The extension cord for the printer had been misplaced, and it took some time to reconfigure the wiring. I had 1 customer and 1 mail order today.

Customer 15A arrived around 11:45, and she did something that no other customer has yet to do… she wrote her purchased word by herself—EARLOBE. In my bafflement, I forgot to turn on the video recording for this customer, so there is no record.

Mail Order Customer 3 ordered my name with my middle initial—Robert M. Fitterman (2 words + 1 letter).

In an effort to do business-related activities when business is slow, I beautified the "Rob's Word Shop" storefront sign from 12:45 to 1:30.

> Customer 15A: EARLOBE
> Mail Order Customer 3: Robert M. Fitterman

Total sales: $3.50

[This transaction has no written or video record as I forgot to turn on computer. Through the receipt records, however, I have been able to recover the customer's word: EARLOBE. Customer 15A assumed that Rob's Word Shop was modeled like a workshop and she wrote her own word, choosing her materials from the shop's selection.]

DAY 7

Ledger

Left apartment at 10:53 walking. Stopped for coffee. Arrived at Rob's Word Shop at 11:03 AM. Set up between 11:10-11:20. Probably my busiest day to date.

Customer 16 arrived at 11:30. He ordered the 2 words—Robert Fitterman—and asked for them as a signature. I produced this signature on 4 separate pieces of paper (pen, marker, print & script) but only charged for the 2 letters. Customer 16 also asked for quotation marks on a separate piece of paper (all punctuation marks are free.) Lastly, Customer 16 ordered the word Pichler in cursive as a signature. For this last order, the customer produced his own sheet of paper that already had the word pichler printed on it. $3 total.

Customer 17 arrived at 12:15 PM and ordered the words: Don't make YOUR problem MY problem. The charge was for 5 words because "problem" is repeated. The words were written in lowercase cursive marker except for the pronouns: "Your" and "My" which were written in uppercase block letters. $5.

Customer 18 ordered 6 words: manufactured scarcity as a phrase on a single sheet of paper, retarded practice as a phrase on a single sheet of paper, the word I (single sheet), and the word ressentiment (single sheet). This customer received a 20% employee discount, which made the total $4.80.

Customer 19 ordered 2 words: under and where? on a single piece of paper in marker and written in cursive. $2.

Customer 20 ordered 3 letters on separate pieces of paper: I, K, and E. These were written in marker, all uppercase and centered on the page. $1.50.

Customer 21 ordered 2 words as a phrase on a single sheet: oil'd pelican. We arrived at these words together. They were written in lowercase cursive with marker. The word oil'd was offered free of charge as a student discount. $1.

Customer 22 ordered the words flowers and ICE—flowers appeared on a separate sheet of paper; it was written in quotes (gratis), lowercase cursive with marker. ICE was written in all caps with marker. $2.

Total sales: $19.30

Left Rob's Word Shop at 2:20 PM; stopped at stationary store for folders, new marker, 2 Sales Books, and a computer printer cartridge. Total price $48.70. Arrived at apartment at 2:45 PM. Received a phone message requesting "Gift Certificates." Designed 2 $1 Gift Certificates and sent to patron as an attachment file via email. The Gift Certificate customers never came to the store to redeem their gifts, and the balance due from this customer who requested the Gift Certificates is still outstanding.

Customer 16

CUSTOMER 16: quotation marks

ROB: quotation marks as a… as a word or as the actual mark?

CUSTOMER 16: uh, I'm not sure… I'm not even sure if it's one letter or two… you tell me

ROB: ok… here's the exciting news that I have for you and it's especially exciting because you said what's the special today… all marks of punctuation are free… there's no charge for marks of punctuation!… so we can think about that and we can think about the word… there're two words… quotation marks is two words…

CUSTOMER 16: hmm

ROB: but then there is just " "(quotation marks), which are free

CUSTOMER 16: yeah, that's what I want

ROB: that's what you want?

CUSTOMER 16: either free or not

ROB: they are free… quotation marks are free, so you… you, um, so let's start there and you still get to make some requests even though they're free… would you like them with a marker, a pen, or a printer?

CUSTOMER 16: um that's up to you

ROB: ok, I like the pen… um, would you like them horizontal or vertical?

CUSTOMER 16: in the air

ROB: in the air… very nice… I have to interpret that, um, in the air… and would you like them large or small or medium or my choice?

CUSTOMER 16: uh, any is fine

ROB: any is fine... ok, here we go... feeling confident now

CUSTOMER 16: I'm getting into this, I think I'll purchase more stuff

ROB: that's it... happens to some of my, uh, finest customers... they thought they were done and who knows what happens... ok, so... so far you're pleased with your transaction all right? ...very good, now, yeah, you think you might be interested in something else?

CUSTOMER 16: yes I'd like to purchase your signature

ROB: oh very interesting... well, that, um... a very nice thought... so that would be two words

CUSTOMER 16: yes

ROB: I don't use my middle name, um... very good... now we have the same questions... do we want this, uh, in, uh, Sharpie or pen?

CUSTOMER 16: or printed

ROB: or printed... but that's not really a signature so much as...

CUSTOMER 16: ok um...

ROB: so I... I...

CUSTOMER 16: is there a discount if I take both?

ROB: I will... you mean... are they... are they both gonna be on the same page or two different pages?

CUSTOMER 16: different

ROB: two different pages... um, yes, I think... I think you can have two for the price of one on the signatures since they are the same... in fact just... it's the same words so, yeah, we'll tha... that's... that will be fine... we'll do one of each... I like that very much... all right I'm ready

CUSTOMER 16: and printed?

ROB: and printed, printed…

CUSTOMER 16: of course you can refuse

ROB: no, no, no! why would I refuse?

CUSTOMER 16: it's your shop

ROB: such a, uh, no… such a, uh, fair request… ok let's… I'm gonna start with printed… wow!… and requests, um, of what we have… one with marker… we have one with pen and then the printed…

CUSTOMER 16: yes

ROB: …pen or marker… it doesn't matter to you?

CUSTOMER 16: printed… oh I think what does print mean? I thought it's inkjet printer

ROB: no, no, no… ah, we could use the printer as well

CUSTOMER 16: I thought that's what…

ROB: I thought, no, I thought you meant as opposed to cursive

CUSTOMER 16: huh?

ROB: I thought you meant print as opposed to cursive

CUSTOMER 16: ah ok

ROB: so, in other words… but we can do the printer as well… so, in other words, this is… this is just a sample so, in other words… right… so my signature would be something like this… now printed would be something like that… in English we say that is printing and that is script or cursive, so if we use the, uh, the printer we can have something with italics or something just printed

CUSTOMER 16: hmm…

ROB: or I could do this... and this... and then we would have a third one that would basically be this... those are our choices... so should we do three pages and each w... w... repli... replicating?... ok very good... ok so the first one... let's have the first one as a, um, um, just printed and we'll use the marker... ok, how's that for starts?

CUSTOMER 16: that's even a fourth version

ROB: well it... I... I thought this might look better than this... what do you think?

CUSTOMER 16: I like

ROB: you prefer both?

CUSTOMER 16: well it's...

ROB: you might prefer both

CUSTOMER 16: it's your signature

ROB: well it's printed, right? since I'm saying that it's all for the same price right? I think...

CUSTOMER 16: no, uh, I mean well...

ROB: no I think for the sake of symmetry, we should have...

CUSTOMER 16: huh?

ROB: we should have one of each... we should have this one and we should also have it handwritten... I'm getting into the, um, the symmetry of the... these two, ok, let's put these two aside... now we also... what I was getting at... that would be interesting then we would also have one signature... one with pen and one with marker right? so, then, we have... we have this one and then we have this one... ok, good, so now we have four beautiful... you're getting a very good deal because I am committed to the idea that you're still only buying two

CUSTOMER 16: I'll buy more

ROB: all right so we have, uh, 5-19 seems a little redundant to sign these again but after all I'm a man of, uh, order

CUSTOMER 16: I'm getting eight signatures in fact

ROB: that's amazing... nineteen... I like these... they're always backwards

Customer 17

CUSTOMER 17: concerning my position... hey, again, um... are we recording here?

ROB: yeah

CUSTOMER 17: um... well, I said something to... excuse me... let's go a little bit like that... yeah here we go... everything is so [unintelligible]... uh, that struck me as being my potential of... I don't know if mantra's the right word, uh, maxim... not it's... not an aphorism, um, I don't know what it would be, but...

ROB: maxim's a pretty good word

CUSTOMER 17: yeah maxim's not bad

ROB: yeah

CUSTOMER 17: but it... but it was the actual phrase that I said to somebody who was... um... um... long story short is that a very confused curator from Europe wanted to get a bunch of stuff from Anthology for an exhibit, uh, the exhibit is scheduled to open like June somewhere... like fifteenth or twentieth, um, they requested yesterday a, like, laundry list of things... films which don't exist in video formats they want to screen on video, uh, they want to get, uh, you know ten 16mm prints of this one film so they can put it on a looper and have enough copies to, you know, replace it when it breaks down but they basically... they're like a year late on making a request like this and when I told them, like, you... you don't understand, I can't do this, I won't do this, I can't do this and it's not gonna happen... they got really, really frustrated—I got inundated for a couple of days with emails and pleading and how much will it cost and, you know, of course it's not a matter of cost it's a matter of time

ROB: right...

CUSTOMER 17: ...especially since I'm gone in early June and, um, I don't really care... I mean like it's just I can't make anybody's life more difficult, plus it's like you can't accommodate requests... it's impossible

ROB: it's not possible right

CUSTOMER 17: and so they weren't getting this even though the person spoke, you know, very plain and perfect English and so I said something to them which I actually think was both rude enough to make my point clear and really like ended the conversation and I thought that might be a good word to buy... I could own it... I said it, but I need to own it!

ROB: but, yeah, then it could really be yours

CUSTOMER 17: exactly, yeah, yeah...

ROB: see the shop can be very good for that... solidifies an identity... you know, you already feel strongly about this

CUSTOMER 17: yeah, yeah

ROB: beautiful

CUSTOMER 17: and that's why I sort of thought that, like, I don't know if it's a mantra or if it's a catchphrase, a maxim, uh, maybe once I see it on paper I'll have a better idea

ROB: yeah

CUSTOMER 17: but this is the thing…

ROB: your maxim?

CUSTOMER 17: it could be my maxim…

ROB: yeah

CUSTOMER 17: my epitaph… um, I, uh, I thought about this and I, um, I wanna see if it's possible from a financial point of view… I think it's six words but one of the words repeats so…

ROB: that's free

CUSTOMER 17: that's free?

ROB: that's gratis

CUSTOMER 17: so… ok then maybe we're talking about five words that would be the… uh, uh, uh, uh, deal killer… the phrase that I said to them yesterday was: don't make your problem my problem…

ROB: nice…

CUSTOMER 17: …that really shut down all communication and I thought that… that's kinda… I can kinda live by that

ROB: you know you can hang it above your…

CUSTOMER 17: …yeah I really want to frame it and hang it… yeah I kinda think that it's, uh…

ROB: get it engraved in a wood plaque…

CUSTOMER 17: like… I can't do it cause look at the plaque… I wish I could help you but the plaque… yeah, exactly, yeah

ROB: that's very good… I like that very much… ok, good

CUSTOMER 17: so… don't make your problem my problem, and problem repeating twice

ROB: problem repeating... it's a freebie

CUSTOMER 17: yeah but I don't... I mean, uh, I haven't... I would love your input on how to graphically lay this one out

ROB: mm-hmm

CUSTOMER 17: I don't really...

ROB: ok, I would say...

CUSTOMER 17: ...I'm so... I'm too verbally attached to it to visualize it

ROB: yeah?

CUSTOMER 17: ...and personally, emotionally attached

ROB: mm-hmm

CUSTOMER 17: ...because that was like, I think, that was one of the most honest things I've ever said to somebody who was... who was giving me a problem, yeah, in a professional context where I just looked and said: you know, listen...

ROB: yeah, yeah

CUSTOMER 17: and and...

ROB: ...it's kinda your bumper sticker... all right I think... here's what I think...

CUSTOMER 17: for my 1994...

ROB: yep...

CUSTOMER 17: ...Toyota...

ROB: that's right

CUSTOMER 17: yeah

ROB: it's got 1994 written all over it...

CUSTOMER 17: it's kinda the bumper stickler equivalent of, uh, that wonderful t-shirt one can find on Saint Mark's: fuck you you fucking fuck

ROB: yeah, yeah, yeah, or, uh: you have me confused with someone who gives a shit... yeah

CUSTOMER 17: that's good

ROB: yeah

CUSTOMER 17: yeah, yeah, uh, uh, uh: how's my driving? CALL 1-800-EAT-SHIT

ROB: so you're in a... there's a genre there

CUSTOMER 17: right, right, I like that

ROB: you fit right in

CUSTOMER 17: my kid beat up your honor student... or one of those...

ROB: yeah, right, yeah, yeah, now, um... the pen is out because it's not bold enough

CUSTOMER 17: oh yeah, you're right

ROB: the pen...

CUSTOMER 17: ...it's a declarative statement

ROB: so I think we either... we either need a marker or we could go with the printer

CUSTOMER 17: we could go big font

ROB: we could go big font... well, we should go big font on either one, whether it's going to be marker or printed... now the thing that's interesting to me...

CUSTOMER 17: ...all caps?

ROB: either all caps—which would be the obvious choice which I think is good—or kind of frilly cursive which would be more ironic... be like, uh, kind of a home sweet home

CUSTOMER 17: right, right, right, right, right...

ROB: cursive?

CUSTOMER 17: that might be something for a future, uh, tapestry...

ROB: mm-hmm...

CUSTOMER 17: ...type of thing

ROB: mm-hmm... but...

CUSTOMER 17: ...what do you think about mixing... don't make capital your problem capital my lowercase problem... I mean there... there's...

ROB: that's nice... that... that could be very nice, or it could be bold and all cap?

CUSTOMER 17: mmm... or if we were going through the computer, uh, you could go and do it in italics: don't make your problem and then like cap, well, my problem... you know what I mean?

ROB: yeah

CUSTOMER 17: the, the, the, the, the, the other person and the my could be...

ROB: right, as a scrap, let's see...

CUSTOMER 17: let's mock it up

ROB: we could do something like, uh, if we weren't on the... if you had like: don't make... see, it could be like that... your problem...

CUSTOMER 17: oh, I see what you're saying

ROB: right

CUSTOMER 17: yeah, yeah

ROB: ...my problem or the opposite which might make more sense, right, which would be more like...

CUSTOMER 17: oh yeah, yeah, yeah... might make more sense... yeah I have, like, a vague memory of my grandparents having like that written in, like, in... in, um, Yiddish in the bathroom

ROB: right... that's what you're referencing here

CUSTOMER 17: yeah, yeah, yeah, and... but it's like totally knit by my grandfather or something, yeah

ROB: I don't know... these are... these are kind of...

CUSTOMER 17: it's a big decision

ROB: see, yeah, yeah, these are kind of, uh, kind of interesting and then you have the printer, of course, we can do anything... something about the handwritten seems a little more angry

CUSTOMER 17: yeah, I think you're right... I definitely think you're right

ROB: very good maxim to live by... you could really... you know, that could take you far

CUSTOMER 17: got me this far

ROB: there you go

Customers 18, 19, 20

CUSTOMER 18: I have a few... has anyone bought the word I ?

ROB: um, it has been in some phrases I think

CUSTOMER 18: yeah?

ROB: maybe not, though, maybe not... um...

CUSTOMER 19: can you not buy a word that someone else has?

ROB: no, you can... you absolutely can

CUSTOMER 18: yeah

CUSTOMER 19: oh, ok

ROB: in fact, um, let's see I as a phrase, no?

CUSTOMER 18: all right

ROB: no, no one has used... [off] hello!

CUSTOMER 20 [OFF]: hello

ROB [OFF]: how are you?

CUSTOMER 20 [OFF]: good

ROB [OFF]: good, um, just ca... can you have a cup of coffee or something, I'll be... you'll be next?

CUSTOMER 20 [OFF]: well I'm meeting... maybe I can come tomorrow then

ROB [OFF]: yeah, you have fifteen minutes

CUSTOMER 20 [OFF]: ok

ROB [OFF]: yeah we'll only be fifteen minutes

CUSTOMER 18: yeah we won't even be that long

ROB [OFF]: these… these guys

CUSTOMER 18: we'll be very quick

ROB [OFF]: yeah these guys don't want to talk to me very long

CUSTOMER 19: yeah we've been thinking about it

CUSTOMER 20 [OFF]: you've been thinking about what you're gonna buy

CUSTOMER 19: yeah

ROB: yeah

CUSTOMER 18: let's begin

ROB: ok

CUSTOMER 18: I just… I just want the word I

ROB: just the word I ?

CUSTOMER 18: in your hand, just as you would normally write it

ROB: ok, so that is… so you… you… your getting a very good deal because you could actually purchase that as a letter

CUSTOMER 18: no I want the word

ROB: you want the word I ?

CUSTOMER 18: I'm gonna pay the full dollar

ROB: even with your discount?

CUSTOMER 18: and I want it in pen, I don't want it in…

ROB: you don't want marker, you want it in pen

CUSTOMER 18: I want it just as if you had written the word I

105

ROB: ok, uh, cap?

CUSTOMER 18: yeah the word I which is usually capped

ROB: the pronoun I

CUSTOMER 18: yes the word I... there's one word I

ROB: no there's also this i

CUSTOMER 18: well you're not listening...

ROB: ...and would you like...

CUSTOMER 18: ...you're not listening, Rob!

ROB: ...and would you like this, uh, uh, uh, horizontal or vertical?

CUSTOMER 18: how would you normally write it if you were going to write and where would you begin?

ROB: I would begin in the upper left hand corner

CUSTOMER 18: I think that sounds really good

ROB: some customers are really difficult

CUSTOMER 19: yeah

CUSTOMER 18: would you usually... would you write in cursive or in print?

ROB: uh, if it were an I, it would be in print

CUSTOMER 18: all right printed, please, all right

ROB: that's it?

CUSTOMER 18: that's it for that one

CUSTOMER 19: that's great

ROB: stamp on the front or back

CUSTOMER 18: on the front please

ROB: all right... ok

CUSTOMER 18: I would like...

ROB: that's one...

CUSTOMER 18: that's one... I would like the same format

ROB: yes

CUSTOMER 18: manufactured scarcity

ROB: manufactured scarcity... pen or marker?

CUSTOMER 18: pen please... would you write it in pen if you had to write the words manufactured scarcity?

ROB: in the shop? as a... as a suggestion from the shop? or...

CUSTOMER 18: ...it's hard to say

CUSTOMER 19: ...or in real life

ROB: if I were... if I were in real life... 'cause they're not the same in the shop... I would recommend... I'm really liking the Sharpie... uh

CUSTOMER 18: no I don't want that

CUSTOMER 19: anything you ask...

CUSTOMER 18: I think I'm going to have to be the customer...

ROB: ...put your foot down

CUSTOMER 18: I'm putting it

ROB: manufactured scarcity... would you like that in cursive or in print?

CUSTOMER 18: I want it the same as the I... let's do it...

ROB: initial cap?

CUSTOMER 18: initial cap only on manufactured

ROB: man-u-fac-tured, and then scarcity we're gonna have all...

CUSTOMER 18: all lower case

ROB: scarcity with a c right?

CUSTOMER 18: yeah

ROB: all right you got it... uh, vertical?

CUSTOMER 18: yeah portrait

ROB: as I would do it up in the corner, in the same way...

CUSTOMER 18: yeah, yeah, I like that... I feel like I get something that most people don't

ROB: manufactured

CUSTOMER 18: you have really...

ROB: ...scarcity

CUSTOMER 19: ...yeah that's nice

CUSTOMER 18: ...you have great handwriting

CUSTOMER 19: that's really nice

ROB: thank you... ok, so we have, uh, what's today... the nineteenth?

CUSTOMER 18: I have another one

CUSTOMER 20 [OFF]: can I just interrupt one second... are you getting a lot of words?... 'cause I....

CUSTOMER 18: just a few more

CUSTOMER 20 [OFF]: 'cause I know exactly what I want

CUSTOMER 18: I know exactly what I want too

CUSTOMER 20 [OFF]: should I come later?... may I'll come later...

ROB [OFF]: I... I think the whole thing should be...

CUSTOMER 18: this should be done in five minutes

CUSTOMER 20 [OFF]: ok, ok

CUSTOMER 19: yeah

ROB: yeah... yeah

CUSTOMER 20 [OFF]: sorry

ROB: no...

CUSTOMER 20 [OFF]: I just have an appointment, and I was just going to run in here and I was getting a birthday present

ROB: 'cause you're excited

CUSTOMER 20 [OFF]: what?

ROB: 'cause you're excited about getting your word

CUSTOMER 20 [OFF]: yes

ROB [OFF]: we're gonna be quick

CUSTOMER 20 [OFF]: ok

CUSTOMER 18: same thing

ROB: ok

CUSTOMER 18: same form and everything... retarded practice

ROB: retard practice

CUSTOMER 18: -ed!

ROB: e-d ... retard-ed practice

CUSTOMER 18: that's good... I like that

CUSTOMER 19: great

ROB: very nice

CUSTOMER 18: is there one more? I wanted... do you know how to spell the word resentiment? like re-sentiment

ROB: no, we can look it up

CUSTOMER 18: that's the last one I want, yeah, all right one more for me and I'll spell it for you... so... r-e-s-s

ROB: r-e-s-s

CUSTOMER 18: e-n-t-i

ROB: e-n-t-i

CUSTOMER 18: uh, m-e-n-t

ROB: m-e-n-t

CUSTOMER 18: yeah

ROB: ok same place, same everything

CUSTOMER 18: I like it

CUSTOMER 19: you've invented a whole new way of page orientation

ROB: mmm... nice

CUSTOMER 18: yeah

CUSTOMER 19: that is very nice

ROB: nice word

CUSTOMER 18: I think this is some of your best work, Rob

ROB: excellent

CUSTOMER 18: all right I'm done

CUSTOMER 19: I just have one

ROB: ok and we'll do receipts in a minute so we can get to Suzanne as well... just one word?

CUSTOMER 19: no it's two words... and I think I want the Sharpie and I want it in landscape

ROB: Sharpie and landscape... ok...

CUSTOMER 19: under where?... two words w-h-e-r-e with a question mark at the end

ROB: in the middle of the page?

CUSTOMER 18: yeah, oh yeah perfect

ROB: looks good?

CUSTOMER 19: yeah

CUSTOMER 18: very good

ROB: love it... stamp anywhere

CUSTOMER 19: yeah

ROB: this is my usual spot

CUSTOMER 19: looking good

CUSTOMER 18 [OFF]: we can move over, you can have my seat

ROB: uh, or I can just move the video... you guys don't have to get up... ok, so we're gonna have Sharpie or pen?

CUSTOMER 20: Sharpie landscape

ROB: ok, Sharpie landscape

CUSTOMER 20: I want an I

ROB: I... the pronoun I ?

CUSTOMER 20: the letter I

ROB: the letter I

CUSTOMER 20: just an I

ROB: ok

CUSTOMER 20: then I want just a K

ROB: ok

CUSTOMER 20: then I want just an E

ROB: all right just a K

CUSTOMER 20: and just an E

ROB: ...and just an E

CUSTOMER 20: yes

ROB: upper case or lower case?

CUSTOMER 20: I'm sorry... I'm so rushed

ROB: no, no problem... upper case or lower case?

CUSTOMER 20: I want low... upper case

ROB: upper case and, um, any other specifications?

CUSTOMER 20: that's it, but one per page... I'm buying them as letters

ROB: one per page?

CUSTOMER 20: yeah, I'm just... individual letters

ROB: so now the I is becoming a little more popular

CUSTOMER 18: a little more popular... two in one day... that's a good rate, but she bought a letter... I bought a word

CUSTOMER 20: yeah, it's cheaper if you buy the letter

CUSTOMER 18: it is cheaper if you buy the letter

CUSTOMER 19: it was an act of [unintelligable]... it was a...

CUSTOMER 18: mine is a luxury item

CUSTOMER 20: so is tomorrow your last day selling?

ROB: no, no... next week too... ok, so... I, K, E... would you like 'em stamped?

CUSTOMER 20: yes each stamped

CUSTOMER 18: ...you forgot the A

ROB: same place?

CUSTOMER 20: yes

ROB: right... I never thought about that... if you had an A at the end...

CUSTOMER 20: it would be...

ROB: ... i-k-e-a

CUSTOMER 20: IKEA, right

CUSTOMER 19: oh wow

ROB: Ike's probably heard that one

CUSTOMER 20: yeah... it's his birthday today

ROB: oh

CUSTOMER 20: so it's going to say 5-19 on it

ROB: oh perfect

CUSTOMER 18: oh that's good

CUSTOMER 20: he's sixteen

ROB: wow, what a nice sixteenth birthday

CUSTOMER 20: [inaudible] my father-in-law came in today...

ROB: yeah?...

CUSTOMER 20: so we're taking him to buy some words from you tomorrow...

ROB: oh beautiful... beautiful...

CUSTOMER 20: ...that he went to New York to buy some letters and words... he'll be able to dine out on that story for a while

ROB: well I know they get a good kick out of that

CUSTOMER 20: yeah

ROB: "they"... whoever the "they" is

CUSTOMER 20: "those people"

ROB: "those people"... so, yeah, you only spent a dollar fifty

CUSTOMER 20: ..."those people"... our parents

ROB: so you'll be back tomorrow?

CUSTOMER 20: yeah

ROB: here's your, um, receipt

CUSTOMER 20: so I'll owe you a dollar fifty?

ROB: you owe me a buck fifty and I have it in my guest book, so...

CUSTOMER 20: all right

Customers 21, 22

ROB: ok, good, we're on... ok, there you are in all your beauty... great, ok, good... so you're... you're looking for word

CUSTOMER 21: I think [unintelligible]

ROB: you're not entirely sure yet

CUSTOMER 21: I think I'd like it to be a fashionable word

ROB: a fashionable word... all right... um...

CUSTOMER 21: and how much is a word?

ROB: a word is one dollar

CUSTOMER 21: one dollar...

ROB: and letters are fifty cents

CUSTOMER 21: so the words aren't by the letter?

ROB: no, no, no, not at all

CUSTOMER 21: ok

ROB: so a word's a much better deal, in general, unless you feel compelled to...

CUSTOMER 22: you can't do as much with it... seems a little bit...

ROB: yeah that's true, although my best seller is a letter so far

CUSTOMER 22: S ?

ROB: yeah, the letter S

CUSTOMER 22: hmm...

CUSTOMER 21: hmm...

ROB: which you learned about that on the blog?

CUSTOMER 22: I did learn about that on the blog, yeah… I, you know, I do my, uh, my pre-shopping research

ROB: that's it

CUSTOMER 21: I don't want your bestseller… I want…

CUSTOMER 22: [unintelligible] cutting coupons

CUSTOMER 21: I want a word you haven't sold yet

ROB: ok, good, and you want something fashionable

CUSTOMER 21: something fashionable

ROB: not necessarily something trendy, but fashionable

CUSTOMER 21: fashionable, yeah, not, not necessarily trendy

ROB: uh, fashionable like a… uh… like… uh a text message kind of word fashionable?… or fashionable like fashion industry?… or like fashionable in terms of like theory, theoretically, academically, scholarly fashionable?

CUSTOMER 22: how are you trying to show off?

ROB: um… how do you want this?

CUSTOMER 21: um… I would like it to be appropriate for the season

ROB: appropriate for the season, ok

CUSTOMER 21: um… tasteful but not overstated, a little bit extravagant

ROB: ooh, wow

CUSTOMER 21: at the same time…

ROB: …that's a very tall order

CUSTOMER 21: it is, yeah

ROB: and would we want one word to do all of this?

CUSTOMER 21: no it can, if it has to go to more than one word, then I'm open to that

ROB: mm-hmm

CUSTOMER 21: you know I'd [inaudible] to do that

ROB: all right, um... any... do you have any thoughts already that I should work with or you want me to just start [unintelligible] myself?

CUSTOMER 21: well, I don't know... I just thought, I just... what I wanted when I walked in, so I haven't really thought about it ahead of time, um... a nature word would be fine

ROB: nature word... um, um... I went straight to the oil spill

CUSTOMER 21: ok

ROB: but that's not really, you know, pleasant or fashionable not necessarily

CUSTOMER 21: but what uh...

CUSTOMER 22: ...it's topical

ROB: ...but it's topical

CUSTOMER 21: what word relating to the oil spill

ROB: I was thinking of birds

CUSTOMER 21: a bird

ROB: yeah, like a... uh, pelican or a flamingo

CUSTOMER 22: a glazed bird

CUSTOMER 21: pelican is actually very appealing

ROB: pelican's a beautiful word

CUSTOMER 21: it's a beautiful word... should... I... um... should I modify it?

ROB: oiled?...

CUSTOMER 21: oiled pelican, that's what I would like to buy

ROB: you'll buy oiled pelican?

CUSTOMER 22: glaze, yeah

ROB: it's kinda fresh, but kinda sad all at once

CUSTOMER 21: yeah

ROB: now you have your choice of marker a pen or a printer

CUSTOMER 22: do you do cursive and... ah?

ROB: cursive

CUSTOMER 22: I was curious about that... I didn't know if cursive could be split into letters

ROB: yep

CUSTOMER 22: signatures... I was particularly interested in...

ROB: yep, yep, I did some of those today... my own signature

CUSTOMER 21: I would like... uh, marker and just whatever kind of writing comes most naturally to you

ROB: ok... um, landscape or vertical?

CUSTOMER 21: landscape

ROB: good choices... oiled pelican

CUSTOMER 21: oiled pelican

ROB: now we can have oil apostrophe d or just ed...

CUSTOMER 21: I have to defer to you on that... I don't know

ROB: I don't know... the apostrophe 'd ?

CUSTOMER 21: ...that's nice

ROB: ...somehow sounds nice to me

CUSTOMER 21: that's nice... yeah, that's nice... perfect

ROB: very faux French, right?

CUSTOMER 22: yeah, you make your d in a very interesting way

ROB: yeah

CUSTOMER 22: yeah, you do the little guy first, I don't... I guess I do the same... I guess I do the same, yeah, yeah... I felt like in my head... I felt the line first but [unintelligible]

CUSTOMER 21: I'm very happy

ROB: you like it? I quite like it myself... if I do say myself... this is one of the best... now would you like a... usually, there's a stamp on the front, in the corner

CUSTOMER 21: mm-hmm

ROB: does that sound good to you?

CUSTOMER 21: yeah that sounds good

ROB: ok, there's your stamp

CUSTOMER 22: very nice

ROB: all right, very good, and now we have to do a... um, a receipt

CUSTOMER 21: I'm probably gonna get whatever he wants too, so if you want

ROB: so we'll put 'em all on one receipt?

CUSTOMER 22: yeah, yeah, we can put it all together

ROB: sure... all right, we'll hold off on the receipt, great idea

CUSTOMER 21: you talk to him about it, I'm gonna get, uh, a drink... do you want a cup of coffee or anything?

ROB: nah, I just had one, thanks

CUSTOMER 21: do you want a cup of coffee?

CUSTOMER 22: I'd love a cup of coffee, thank you so much

CUSTOMER 21: black?

CUSTOMER 22: uh... yes, yeah

ROB: [unintelligible]

CUSTOMER 22: I was surprised... eh, I'm looking for a couple of things

ROB: yeah

CUSTOMER 22: ...uh... one would be a word of congratulations... we're going to see someone's play on Saturday... not necessarily the word "congratulations"... I'm not... I thought maybe something... something like flowers, but not "flowers"

ROB: mm-hmm

CUSTOMER 22: per the standard theater...

ROB: mm-hmm

CUSTOMER 22: ...gift

ROB: mm-hmm

CUSTOMER 22: um... I don't know any

ROB: well flowers could be pretty interesting, eh, you know, as a word

CUSTOMER 22: mm-hmm

ROB: giving flowers

CUSTOMER 22: yes... yeah, yeah

ROB: they could be in quotes... "flowers" in quotes

CUSTOMER 22: oh I like that

ROB: yeah, should we do that?

CUSTOMER 22: let's go with that

ROB: all right... um, marker?

CUSTOMER 22: I like marker myself

ROB: the marker... the marker...

CUSTOMER 22: and this is... this is just beautiful

ROB: something along those lines

CUSTOMER 22: whatever's natural... I like the natural...

ROB: "flowers" needs a little flourish, I think, maybe... how's that?

CUSTOMER 22: nice, nice, do you ever have... um, not remainders, but, you know, I worked in an ice cream store for years and you make a mistake and you eat it and you get to a point where you're like making mistakes, you know

ROB: I have... it's funny you should say that because I, I, I, I, want to redo this, on the r, but you know, I had a stack over here earlier... um, but no I'm... I'm the... the... there was a customer just came in... that was a mistake and I said: you can take that, I'm gonna throw it away... and he was very happy...

CUSTOMER 22: ...oh nice

ROB: ...to have two versions

CUSTOMER 22: the quotes is really a nice touch, thank you for that

ROB: I like this a lot

CUSTOMER 22 [OFF]: I got "flowers" for Cici, for the play

CUSTOMER 21: mm, that's nice

CUSTOMER 22: um...

ROB: ok

CUSTOMER 22: and I was also looking for something... I'm not sure... the word hot sprung to mind suddenly but I fear that it's based on seeing that advertisement, that Bruce Nauman advertisement on the subway many times of, like, hands polishing the word "hot" from the MoMA exhibit or something like that

ROB: oh yeah

CUSTOMER 22: you know what I'm talking about

ROB: now I do, yes

CUSTOMER 22: ...and I think that that's what it was... so maybe I'm... I'd rather not be swayed by, by, by advertising

ROB: you can, you can... you can have yours be cold

CUSTOMER 22: that's true yeah let's... let's, um, summer's coming up maybe... how 'bout ice?

ROB: ice... um

CUSTOMER 21: did "flowers" go wrong?

CUSTOMER 22: yeah

ROB: I didn't think that I wasn't happy with the r

CUSTOMER 22: I was surprised... I mentioned to him mistakes and it turned out that was one

ROB: yeah… oh, but you can have that one if you want it

CUSTOMER 22: I would love that one… yeah

ROB: that… that's an example of something that was going to go right into the garbage, so this is uh…

CUSTOMER 22: that's why I was curious if you take them home for yourself

ROB: no it will go in the garbage but what we'll do is we'll write on this one, um… "gratis"

CUSTOMER 22: ah, thank you

ROB: ok, put that one… you never know, you can't have too many "flowers"

CUSTOMER 22: yeah

ROB: ice um… any, uh, specifications or would you like me to do…

CUSTOMER 22: hmm…

ROB: I'm seeing something, I'll tell you what I'm seeing… uh… printed all caps

CUSTOMER 22: I like that

ROB: see that

CUSTOMER 22: yeah, absolutely

ROB: kinda thick…

CUSTOMER 22: yeah

ROB: middle of the page

CUSTOMER 22: um, ICE, um yeah, yeah, centered

ROB: do we like, uh, marks on the top and bottom of the I ?

CUSTOMER 22: this is looking nice

ROB: you like it just like that?

CUSTOMER 22: I like the... uh...

ROB: the serif I guess that would be

CUSTOMER 22: yeah... exactly...

ROB: no serif, sans serif, I like it a lot

CUSTOMER 22: cheers, thank you very much

ROB: yes indeed

CUSTOMER 21: I couldn't be happier with my oil'd pelican

CUSTOMER 22: yeah, that is beautiful

ROB: it's so French [unintelligible]

DAY 8

Ledger

Left apartment on bicycle at 10:50 AM. Arrived at Rob's Word Shop at 10:58 AM. Set up was completed by 11:10. From 11:15-11:30, I worked on the blog post from the day before.

Customers 23 and 24 arrived around 11:30. I spoke at length with Customer 24 about his situation so that I could arrive at a phrase. The phrase we agreed upon was french class girlfriend. He seemed very pleased with his phrase, which was hand-written in cursive, lowercase.

Customer 23 had many orders to fill—all of the words and phrases were provided by the customer. He ordered 12 words, each in marker on separate sheets of paper. Here is the list of Customer 23's words:

> PORTRAIT
> LANDSCAPE
> BUDDHA
> Wife
> Supernatural
> The
> Daughter
> A
> Rubber
> Baby
> Bottle
> Nipple

Customer 25 arrived an hour later and ordered the word divine. He requested that I write it with my eyes closed and left-handed.

Total sales: $16.00

Customers 23, 24

ROB: ok, good, all right... so... um, we're... we're gonna start with your father because we've already started the conversation about what's possible

CUSTOMER 23: ok, great

ROB: is that good? is that ok for you?

CUSTOMER 23: so I'm gonna be on the video just listening to you talk?

ROB: yeah...

CUSTOMER 23: ...to my dad? ok, great

ROB: yeah, yeah, yeah, right yeah, but...

CUSTOMER 23: ...so great

ROB: ...most of it's just audio, anyway, like I said, so...

CUSTOMER 23: ... cool...

ROB: ...so, we're talking about potential... um... paper here... get my materials... yeah, you should have a card free

CUSTOMER 23: thanks

ROB: ok, so we're talking about having the right thing for uh... your French class girlfriend, which I think, by the way, that combination wouldn't be too bad... french class girlfriend... as a phrase

CUSTOMER 24: I like that

ROB: you like that?

CUSTOMER 24: yeah

ROB: I kinda like that too... um, ok, good, let's go with french class girlfriend... now we could hyphenate french class so that you get a discount, one word or it's gonna be three words french class girlfriend... girlfriend is, of course, one word... it's up to you

CUSTOMER 23: I... I... I like the idea that the words are separate

ROB: mm-hmm

CUSTOMER 23: because then you don't know if french class goes together or class girlfriend goes together

CUSTOMER 24: precisely my [inaudible]...

ROB: mmm... so it's all one, it should be all one line too

CUSTOMER 24: yeah

CUSTOMER 23: could be

ROB: that ambiguity...

CUSTOMER 23: could be... that's right

ROB: all right... good... now you have three choices of how this is going to be, uh, manifested: pen, Sharpie, or the printer... which would just be a regular computer print

CUSTOMER 24: oh, ok... Sharpie

ROB: absolutely... good

CUSTOMER 23: it's gotta be Sharpie

ROB: good pick

CUSTOMER 23: gotta be Sharpie

ROB: the Sharpie is the most popular...

CUSTOMER 23: ...yeah

ROB: ...choice for good reason

CUSTOMER 23: yeah

ROB: all right, good... now we have a couple of other interesting things we need to think about... do we want it cursive or printed?

CUSTOMER 24: oh cursive

ROB: cursive, good choice... and do we want it all lower case or initial cap?

CUSTOMER 24: uh all lowercase

ROB: all lower case french class girlfriend... I like the way this is going to look... and then we have to decide do we want it horizontal landscape or vertical on the page?

CUSTOMER 23: horizontal

CUSTOMER 24: ok maybe you can slightly angle...

ROB: slightly angled... sure you mean like, uh, like that?... like across?... like that maybe?

CUSTOMER 24: yeah something like that, no?

CUSTOMER 23: don't do it... you'll regret it... it seems like right now you feel like ok, I'm jaunty, I'm experimental, I'm living on the edge, but then when you put it on your wall it's gonna make you see...

CUSTOMER 24: it'll look like I have to move it

ROB: yeah, make it straight

CUSTOMER 23: yeah, I like it... I don't even think you even need to practice anymore... I think that's it

CUSTOMER 24: yeah

ROB: beautiful

CUSTOMER 23: I think that looks really nice

ROB: now you get... perfect... you get a stamp, um, and that could be on the front or the back, your choice, it's a stamp of that... looks like this... that's the name of the shop

CUSTOMER 23: like the card

ROB: just like the card... most people get it in the corner

CUSTOMER 24: ok

ROB: gives it some you know... good... satisfied?

CUSTOMER 24: perfect

CUSTOMER 23: I love it!... I think it looks really good

CUSTOMER 24: yeah

ROB: good... ok, and for you sir?

CUSTOMER 23: ok, I got a bunch of things

ROB: oh, terrific, ok

CUSTOMER 23: ok, so you know Suzanne was here yesterday right, and she got the letters for Ike's birthday right, and, of course, you remember, cause I think you were here right?... this was where Ike's bar mitzvah was...

ROB: exactly, right

CUSTOMER 23: ...at Bowery Poetry Club

ROB: did he get his, uh, letters yet?

CUSTOMER 23: he loved them

ROB: he loved them?

CUSTOMER 23: he got the letters last night... we had a big party, he got the letters, he loved them

ROB: I'm so happy

CUSTOMER 23: Suzanne framed them individually so…

ROB: beautiful

CUSTOMER 23: they look really spectacular

ROB: that's great

CUSTOMER 23: yeah, part of the reason why we're back here with more orders is not just cause she owed you money, but also because now everybody wants one

ROB: you're here because you're happy with the service

CUSTOMER 23: yeah, we're ecstatic

ROB: nothing makes me happier

CUSTOMER 23: ok um… now… um Suzanne on five separate sheets of paper…

ROB: mm-hmm, let me get some more paper

CUSTOMER 23: ok, you're gonna need a lot of paper here, ok?

ROB: no problem

CUSTOMER 23: so this must be very popular right?… people come in and they chat with you and…

ROB: it's getting more popular everyday

CUSTOMER 23: really?

ROB: yeah

CUSTOMER 23: how long have you been doing it?

ROB: I'm doing it for the month of May

CUSTOMER 23: oh

ROB: so the first day was, what, the fourth of May or something

CUSTOMER 23: uh huh

ROB: it's been going great

CUSTOMER 23: that's great

ROB: yeah, yeah, yeah, yeah

CUSTOMER 23: it's really...

ROB: ...I've got mail orders to fill...

CUSTOMER 23: yeah

ROB: I'm a very busy guy

CUSTOMER 23: that's great

ROB: ...I got a blog to keep up... yeah...

CUSTOMER 23: yeah?

CUSTOMER 24: American small business owner

CUSTOMER 23: yeah

ROB: yeah

CUSTOMER 23: that's fantastic, um, ok the first one is...

CUSTOMER 24: in fact, that's a good phrase

ROB: that's a very good phrase, that's a very good phrase

CUSTOMER 23: there you go... for when you decide to write words for yourself

ROB: gratis

CUSTOMER 23: yeah, right, oh right in that case don't do it, if no one's paying you

CUSTOMER 24: we'll tip him a dollar to support...

CUSTOMER 23: yeah, um, she would like them on five separate sheets of paper: a / rubber / baby / bottle / and nipple

ROB: mmm… all right

CUSTOMER 23: block letters

ROB: mm-hmm

CUSTOMER 23: um, all caps

ROB: mm-hmm

CUSTOMER 23: um, uh, landscape

ROB: mm-hmm

CUSTOMER 23: …and centered like that

ROB: beautiful

CUSTOMER 23: ok, so let's start with that

ROB: ok

CUSTOMER 23: and by the time you're done with that…

ROB: a / rubber / baby…

CUSTOMER 23: a / rubber / baby / bottle / and nipple

ROB: mm-hmm

CUSTOMER 23: and by the time you're done with that, I'll have some others for you

ROB: great… ok…

CUSTOMER 23: ok

ROB: so you have…

CUSTOMER 23: this is twelve and three, that's fifteen bucks

ROB: fifteen bucks

CUSTOMER 23: do I get a stamp?

ROB: absolutely, I almost forgot… now we do these up on the top so you, uh…

CUSTOMER 23: yeah

ROB: and you get for that same price a folder

CUSTOMER 23: oh, fantastic

ROB: so that you don't have to, uh, worry about bending up your…

CUSTOMER 23: …that's great

ROB: …things

CUSTOMER 23: I don't know

ROB: you can each have a folder, you want to have your own folder or you wanna put 'em in this folder?

CUSTOMER 23: I think you need your own folder

CUSTOMER 24: I think I need my own folder

CUSTOMER 23: you're gonna need your own folder

ROB: I got it

CUSTOMER 24: so I can transport it

ROB: I like to put the stamp here if that's all right…

CUSTOMER 23: love it

ROB: comes out very nice on these yellow folders

CUSTOMER 23: it does… it really pops

ROB: "pops" is the right word

CUSTOMER 24: that makes an excellent gift package

CUSTOMER 23: that's right

ROB: well I hope so

CUSTOMER 24: if nothing else it's…

CUSTOMER 23: …I love it… "Nimitz class destroyer"

CUSTOMER 24: what?

CUSTOMER 23: that's what it reminded me of because it's french class girlfriend… the class can also be like "Nimitz class destroyer" or, you know, it's very funny

ROB: thank you

CUSTOMER 23: so…

ROB: I hope you feel like you've gotten your money's worth

CUSTOMER 23: I'm ecstatic… I have to say

ROB: uh huh

CUSTOMER 23: I really have enjoyed this

ROB: I'm so glad

CUSTOMER 23: I think it's a really great project and…

ROB: …thanks

CUSTOMER 23: …you know I'm not done… I may not be done…

ROB: you may not be done and you'll hear more about it, I'm sure

CUSTOMER 23: yeah, well, let me know

ROB: pleasure… pleasure to meet you

CUSTOMER 24: good seeing you

ROB: yeah

CUSTOMER 23: this was really great, Rob, thanks

ROB: I'm so glad… I'm so glad you came by… thank you, it was a real pleasure

CUSTOMER 23: no, I'm really happy

ROB: yay

CUSTOMER 23: I'm really happy

ROB: good, all right

CUSTOMER 23: it's a really great project

ROB: thank you and we'll get together soon

CUSTOMER 23: I really hope so

ROB: yeah

CUSTOMER 23: ok, see you later

ROB: all right, bye

CUSTOMER 23: bye

ROB: super pleasure… thanks

Customer 25

ROB: there you are

CUSTOMER 25: wow!

ROB: looking good

CUSTOMER 25: I guess... not as good as you

ROB: all right... good so, um, I'll tell you how this works you... oh, we decided when we were talking about this last night you wanted to co-create a word maybe right?

CUSTOMER 25: uh, yeah

ROB: yeah, you got it... um, so we have a... you have a choice of a word, a letter, or a phrase

CUSTOMER 25: oh...

ROB: uh, words are one dollar and letters are fifty cents... most people get a word or two words, but some people have gone all out, and all kinds of crazy things...

CUSTOMER 25: all right

ROB: it's [inaudible] your choice

CUSTOMER 25: how much is a phrase?

ROB: you're thinking about a phrase?

CUSTOMER 25: no, no, not really, I was just wondering...

ROB: what's it... what did you... what was the question? did I miss it?

CUSTOMER 25: how much is a...

ROB: oh how... it's, uh, it's, it's still one dollar a word

CUSTOMER 25: ah, one dollar a word, ok

ROB: so if you got, you know, a two-word phrase [inaudible]

CUSTOMER 25: ok

ROB: um... so what are you thinking about?

CUSTOMER 25: like in terms of...

ROB: in a general way so we can start to [inaudible]…

CUSTOMER 25: let's do… words

ROB: let's do words, all right, any particular… ah?

CUSTOMER 25: uh…

ROB: anything on your mind?

CUSTOMER 25: divine

ROB: divine

CUSTOMER 25: yeah

ROB: great word

CUSTOMER 25: it's a very great word

ROB: yeah, ok, so you want to do something with divine?… it goes with something else? or you like… maybe you're gonna like the idea of just divine by itself

CUSTOMER 25: so when I pay for a word, do I just pay for…

ROB: oh, ok, so, good, so I should explain that part

CUSTOMER 25: yeah

ROB: well, when you pay for a word or we decide on this together, we print it…

CUSTOMER 25: ok

ROB: …in few different ways we could do this, we traditionally most of [inaudible] handwritten…

CUSTOMER 25: ok

ROB: so… and then it gets stamped and signed and all this stuff, um… it can be done in a marker…

CUSTOMER 25: ok

ROB: ...it can be done with a pen... it can be done on the computer with the printer...

CUSTOMER 25: ok

ROB: or, in fact, it can not be written at all and just appear digitally on the blog

CUSTOMER 25: um, ok

ROB: which I think is the least fun choice for the customer because you don't get to take anything home

CUSTOMER 25: uh... the screen went black is it still recording?

ROB: yeah

CUSTOMER 25: oh ok

ROB: yeah it's still recording... all right good... so, uh, so we could just do divine or we could think about whether you want divine with something else

CUSTOMER 25: mmm... I think adding something else might limit it... might limit [inaudible]...

ROB: ...adding something else will?

CUSTOMER 25: like adding another word to it?

ROB: yeah, will ruin it?

CUSTOMER 25: yeah... well it might limit our options

ROB: it might limit our options

CUSTOMER 25: yeah, divine can mean a lot of things right now

ROB: right... exactly... don't add anything

CUSTOMER 25: yeah

ROB: I like that... all right, good, so if we go with divine what do you want it to look like between marker, pen...

CUSTOMER 25: oh marker

ROB: printed, marker

CUSTOMER 25: marker's cool

ROB: now we can experiment too... we can try a couple of different things, if you don't like it...

CUSTOMER 25: yeah

ROB: ...you can, you know, you don't have to pay for it

CUSTOMER 25: yeah

ROB: so yeah, I've had a lot of experiments this morning... in fact I had a very particular customer, they, uh, they didn't like a couple of different things so, ok, so as an example we have to think about now, would you want it printed or in script?

CUSTOMER 25: what, what do you mean?

ROB: so... printed like a block like divine or like cursive?

CUSTOMER 25: are you gonna do all that with the marker?

ROB: mm-hmm... well, let's do... let's do a sample

CUSTOMER 25: better yet, you have to do it with your eyes closed

ROB: you want me to do it with my eyes closed?

CUSTOMER 25: and... your left hand

ROB: oh, ha! I love this... see, now [unintelligible] there's something new... never been asked to do that before... ok, so it's divine with my eyes closed, left hand

CUSTOMER 25: yeah, yeah, yeah

ROB: all right would you like it upper case or lower case?

CUSTOMER 25: uh, doesn't matter

ROB: doesn't matter?

CUSTOMER 25: whatever your left hand feels inspired to do

ROB: all right, here we go

CUSTOMER 25: cool

ROB: that is sweet

CUSTOMER 25: that is cool, I like that… I did this, I did, uh, I experimented with blind film-making a couple of weeks ago

ROB: and…?

CUSTOMER 25: it was strange

ROB: this is very nice… I like this a lot… so, typically I then, um, put the stamp of the store on the front in the corner, does that sound good to you?

CUSTOMER 25: yeah

ROB: all right there it is… I like that a lot, let's show the, uh, let's show the camera what we're talking about here, what we're all excited about, there it is!

CUSTOMER 25: there it is!

ROB: that was a great suggestion… see no one's given me any instructions like that before, I like that

CUSTOMER 25: yeah, it's very important

ROB: all right, now good we have to give you a receipt

CUSTOMER 25: ok, can I give you a dollar?

ROB: …and you give me a dollar and we have had a transaction…

ok, so we got uh, five, ten, and you got one word, uh, divine, um, and I think I'm gonna have to write here, uh, "blindfolded"... such a good idea, um, "left handed"... ok, this is... [inaudible] ok, now would you like a folder or an envelope to take this home?

CUSTOMER 25: uh, does it matter?

ROB: well with a folder, I don't have to fold it... depends on what you feel like carrying... an envelope is...

CUSTOMER 25: a folder's fine

ROB: ...is easier to move around, all right, folder it is

CUSTOMER 25: yeah I didn't want to ruin it

ROB: that's the way I think about it, but, yeah... the customer's always right... I'm hoping I got change for a five, I don't know if I do [inaudible]... ok that's yours, um...

CUSTOMER 25: where do you get one of these things?

ROB: I ordered mine online, but we can...

CUSTOMER 25: how much?

ROB: I don't know it's like, uh, thirty bucks, I think twenty five bucks... you can get them, though, on, um, Eleventh Street... there's a guy that makes 'em... customized stamps... East Eleventh between, uh, First and Second, something like that... all right, terrific, let me close this guy...

DAY 9

Ledger:

Left apartment at 10:48 on bicycle and arrived at 10:56. "My Business Hours" sign had fallen down and it took some effort to re-affix it to the window. Set-up from 11:00-11:15.

Customer 26 arrived around 12:15 and purchased the word Simulacra. He asked for the word to be written on the title page of the book he came in with: Philip K. Dick's The Simulacra.

Customer 27 made 3 purchases: pronoun, the madness of decision, :P for a total of $5.50. Customer 27 asked about bartering a musical composition for the words and letters, and I agreed.

Customer 28 purchased the word puella and she asked to have it printed from the computer.

Total sales: $2.00 (+ $5.50 in the barter exchange).

Customer 26

ROB: ok, good, so this is like that, that looks… oh, wow, I love that, in the background that looks perfect, all right good, ok, so, um, how can I help you?… what are you thinking about?

CUSTOMER 26: well I told you the story of my Susan B. Anthony, and I was sitting here reading this book, so I thought I would get you to write this word on this book… physically

ROB: the… the word?

CUSTOMER 26: simulacra

ROB: simulacra

CUSTOMER 26: 'cause I only have one dollar

ROB: on the book itself?

CUSTOMER 26: on the book itself

ROB: …instead of on a separate piece of paper?

CUSTOMER 26: yep… yep…

ROB: ok let's think about how we… we have two choices basically, marker…

CUSTOMER 26: fine marker

ROB: …or pen?

CUSTOMER 26: that's a fine marker, you know, I like that Sharpie

ROB: the Sharpie's been treating me real well

CUSTOMER 26: and I would like the, uh, the, uh, bleeding through

ROB: uh-huh

CUSTOMER 26: I guess, um, I wonder which title page we should...

ROB: you got a lot of choices there

CUSTOMER 26: ...we should use, I think, this one

ROB: I feel like the bleed...

CUSTOMER 26: ...it can bleed through yeah

ROB: we'll do our best to bleed through all right... good... now a couple of choices... do we want this, uh, cursive or print?

CUSTOMER 26: um...

ROB: or make me choose... cursive? print? or make me choose?

CUSTOMER 26: yeah

ROB: one choice...

CUSTOMER 26: you choose

ROB: ok, the next choice is placement on page... you can make me choose, you can choose if you want it over this... under... all the way under...

CUSTOMER 26: um... I'd say, over the word

ROB: over the word, this is gonna be very beautiful... which has a nice ring, right?... the simulacra

CUSTOMER 26: right, that's sort of the idea, I realized I was getting an artwork for a dollar

ROB: right... now I have to be careful here because I don't, I can't practice on the, uh, on how much room I have right?

CUSTOMER 26: mm-hmm... fantastic

ROB: nice huh...

CUSTOMER 26: fantastic

ROB: ok good, now typically I use a stamp... would you like a stamp?

CUSTOMER 26: yes by all means

ROB: this is great that you provided this and... right under, or all the way on the bottom?

CUSTOMER 26: um... perhaps right under... uh...

ROB: I think that would look really nice

CUSTOMER 26: fantastic

ROB: there you go

CUSTOMER 26: [unintelligible] fantastic

ROB: we gotta show this in case we don't get the opportunity later... simulacra on "simulacra"... beautiful now you get a receipt for that... all right you got, oh, I think you got a very good... you got a good word... you got a lot of bang for your buck, I think

CUSTOMER 26: absolutely... especially since this dollar cost me twenty-five cents, that's what I'm talking about

ROB: ok, so we got one word and that's one of my favorite words, not to be prejudiced... for one dollar, one dollar... now you get one more, oh you don't even have... you see now... usually now I offer... whether you... would like a, uh, an envelope or folder... but you don't need it, you got a...

CUSTOMER 26: yeah this goes in the book

ROB: exactly

CUSTOMER 26: you know things really rarely fall out of a book... usually I stash a little money in there... Metrocard...

ROB: that's interesting

148

CUSTOMER 26: I think people would be wary that…

ROB: …it's like a wallet

CUSTOMER 26: …valuable things would fall out…

ROB: …yeah

CUSTOMER 26: …but absolutely not

ROB: yeah, yeah, very good, very secure, all right, very good… so, um, I hope you're satisfied?

CUSTOMER 26: totally

Customer 27

ROB: computer generated… Sharpie… this is my favorite

CUSTOMER 27: ok

ROB: this… I… this is a new edition as a tool

CUSTOMER 27: yeah

ROB: this is a fine marker which I don't personally… I'm not so crazy about…

CUSTOMER 27: ok

ROB: …and then pen

CUSTOMER 27: ok

ROB: so, those are the… those are the tools

CUSTOMER 27: right, right, right

ROB: and then there's all kinds of decisions we have to make about paper and stuff like that

CUSTOMER 27: ok

ROB: yeah

CUSTOMER 27: ok, well, I guess the other... this... I was wondering is...

ROB: mm-hmm

CUSTOMER 27: ...if you've done any trades?

ROB: a barter system?

CUSTOMER 27: yeah

ROB: yes

CUSTOMER 27: I'm just curious

ROB: I have... I have done a couple

CUSTOMER 27: yeah

ROB: yes, yeah, yeah... what do you have in mind?

CUSTOMER 27: I don't know, I'm trying to think what I have that might be of use to you

ROB: uh-huh

CUSTOMER 27: um... I don't know... I could write a song

ROB: I think that... I think that would be great... I think maybe, uh, yeah, maybe we would have to [unintelligible] music or something of a sound piece

CUSTOMER 27: there we go

ROB: maybe even for this video

CUSTOMER 27: yeah

ROB: that's fantastic

CUSTOMER 27: I might be able to do something useful

ROB: ok, you're on

CUSTOMER 27: ok [inaudible]

ROB: that's a deal

CUSTOMER 27: oh… awesome

ROB: I love it!… the best barter of the whole project so far

CUSTOMER 27: of the whole… ok… great

ROB: yeah, it's fantastic

CUSTOMER 27: awesome, um, ok, good so… so, yeah, I have a phrase I was curious about… an emoticon… then I also have a friend who saw I posted something about this on facebook

ROB: yeah?

CUSTOMER 27: and I have a friend who I don't know very well but has decided that you're on his list of people he should meet at some point in his life now

ROB: in his life… oh…

CUSTOMER 27: so I thought it might be nice to get him a gift

ROB: beautiful

CUSTOMER 27: but I'm not sure what… so I thought maybe I could get some advice from you on that

ROB: um… well we could think of that maybe together

CUSTOMER 27: ok

ROB: or some more about that… ok… good, let me see… let me get… so, let's start from the beginning

CUSTOMER 27: ok

ROB: so you had a phrase in mind?

CUSTOMER 27: yeah

ROB: for starts, ok... and do you have an idea of whether you want it printed or handwritten?

CUSTOMER 27: no—I didn't know what my options would be

ROB: exactly... right...

CUSTOMER 27: now I have to figure it out?

ROB: now that you're here...

CUSTOMER 27: ...right...

ROB: ...everything changes... we're still there?... good, ok, um... what's the phrase?

CUSTOMER 27: the madness of decision

ROB: oooh... very nice... do you want to see... we... we can do a test run... we can see what it looks like

CUSTOMER 27: ok

ROB: as an, um... and then we can decide if we like this

CUSTOMER 27: yeah... you're the professional, so however you think is best

ROB: see?... I... I do need a... a staff... hello... yeah, my staff is very short... ok... the madness of decision

CUSTOMER 27: yeah

ROB: ok that's one possibility

CUSTOMER 27: awesome

ROB: it would look like that

CUSTOMER 27: yeah

ROB: do you like that?

CUSTOMER 27: yeah I do

ROB: ok, good, then what happens next is that I stamp it and sign it and consider that one done

CUSTOMER 27: awesome

ROB: so excited about this barter idea, I just haven't done enough of it

CUSTOMER 27: I'm so glad

ROB: love it... there you go

CUSTOMER 27: thank you

Customer 28

CUSTOMER 28: um, where's your camera?

ROB: it's right here

CUSTOMER 28: oh

ROB: it's in the...

CUSTOMER 28: oh, I see, yep, well...

ROB: it's gonna go off in a minute anyway, you won't see anything you won't ...

CUSTOMER 28: I can't look at it

ROB: ...see yourself

CUSTOMER 28: but, um, I'll go along with it

ROB: all right good... so what do you got in mind?

CUSTOMER 28: um well, really just one word... puella... it's latin, do you...

ROB: ...dwelluh?

CUSTOMER 28: puella

ROB: puella?

CUSTOMER 28: p-u-e-l-l-a , it's a Latin word... it means "girl"... it's just a word I remember from Latin class

ROB: terrific

CUSTOMER 28: ...and I always liked it 'cause I thought of that ancient time... a girl...

ROB: very nice... puella... uh it's [inaudible] so we have our choices of... there's three basically, three ways that we make words: we have the printer, we have the pen, and we have the Sharpie... I could make all decisions, or you could make all decisions, or we can arrive at them together as to how this is gonna happen... those are the... that's the first thing

CUSTOMER 28: wow, um, I'd like to see what you print out

ROB: from the printer?

CUSTOMER 28: mm-hmm

ROB: you got it... so then we can decide if it's gonna... on the printer... you can decide if you want it landscape or vertical?

CUSTOMER 28: landscape

ROB: landscape... and if you want, well, let's come up... let's go over to the printer... we'll see what we can do... the last, the last, thank you, the last, uh, customer was interested in the printer... ok so, um, cursive or print?

CUSTOMER 28: pardon me

ROB: cursive or print? you like italics or print?

CUSTOMER 28: print

ROB: print, so if it's print what about, um, I like Arial... do you like Arial?

CUSTOMER 28: yeah it's fine

ROB: all right so let's go Arial bold, um, we're landscape, um, initial cap? no initial cap? all caps?

CUSTOMER 28: I think all lowercase

ROB: all lowercase, beautiful... let's see about something like... I think we can go all the way with this one... pretty nice, shall we center it?... ok, I don't know how that's gonna be with the landscape, but we will find out, um, print settings...

CUSTOMER 28: actually, you know, it fits on the page nicely... there... are you gonna sign it?

ROB: I am

CUSTOMER 28: ok, that's good...

ROB: we'll try it

CUSTOMER 28: ...just like it is

ROB: if we don't like it landscape we can always go vertical, see what we find... I'm borrowing this printer... oh yeah, that looks really nice too... and I never know how it behaves, it's sort of like a mystery but it's doing... it does all right and it can do...

CUSTOMER 28: is that gonna feed in there [inaudible]?... look at how it's sitting in there

ROB: yeah I think it's the…

CUSTOMER 28: oh I see, I see

ROB: it's the thing at the back that's [unintelligible] let's see what happened here… here we go

CUSTOMER 28: I didn't know this place was open for lunch, is it always?

ROB: it is… this is, um…

CUSTOMER 28: …there's [inaudible] or something

ROB: …there was a big [inaudible]

CUSTOMER 28: …you're almost done with it, this week, with this store?… are you gonna move your store somewhere else?

ROB: no I'm not, I'm done… the project's…

CUSTOMER 28: …farmer's markets?

ROB: nope, the project is gonna be done… now I don't know why we're having problems printing here

CUSTOMER 28: it says it's printing

ROB: I don't know… it does, but it's not… oh it's offline… silly… that'll do it

CUSTOMER 28: …it's Brian… it's Brian who was like David's childhood friend… David Wojnarowicz

ROB: yeah

CUSTOMER 28: they were… they went to like high school together and…

ROB: that's really funny

CUSTOMER 28: ...when I... the day I met Brian, I met... or a week after... I met Dirk... he introduced me to David and Brian... wow that's nice...

ROB: good

CUSTOMER 28: yeah

ROB: all right, did you see the show at NYU?... we don't really need this... at the NYU gallery?...

CUSTOMER 28: mm-hmm

ROB: Is... is it interesting? I only saw the, you know, the outside... all right we can turn this off...

DAY 10

Ledger:

Left apartment at 10:51 on bicycle and arrived at shop around 10:56. Set-up was very quick and easy between 11:00-11:10 AM.

Customer 29 arrived around 11:20 and purchased the following sentence: Are you going to the Guggenheim for the Buckminster Fuller film, or what? We arrived at this phrase together—it was part of a short prose portrait by the customer. Total count 13 words, $13.00. Because Customer 29 had purchased over $10 worth of goods, I offered a free letter, word or phrase. The free phrase he chose was kimono clooney, which is also related to his prose portraits.

Customer 30 arrived around 11:45 and chose the word poetic. We tried it both as all caps printed and as lowercase script. We both agreed that the first choice looked better, but I offered the other gratis. Total sale: $1.

I also filled 3 mail orders:

    Mail Order Customer 4: die möglichkeiten $2
    Mail Order Customer 5: antique / grandmother / short $3
    Mail Order Customer 6: Frame This / Pipe Down [gratis] $2

Total sales: $21.00; amount received $13.00.

Customer 29

CUSTOMER 29: so I choose a word, letter, phrase of my own choosing from wherever I pick it out of my brain?

ROB: right

CUSTOMER 29: and then I give that phrase or word to you?

ROB: right

CUSTOMER 29: and then you do something with it?

ROB: I write it

CUSTOMER 29: you write it?

ROB: yeah, but, actually I've had clients who prefer to write it themselves… um…

CUSTOMER 29: so you write the actual phrase down?

ROB: right… right… or I arrive at a phrase for you… it's your choice

CUSTOMER 29: oh

ROB: or we arrive at a phrase together

CUSTOMER 29: ok, so I can…

ROB: …those are all possibilities

CUSTOMER 29: so I can give you a phrase…

ROB: mm-hmm

CUSTOMER 29: and then if I ask you to give me another phrase, you'll give me something back right?

ROB: yeah

CUSTOMER 29: ok

ROB: yeah that's what happened with Dirk and I, in fact, he had a word, uh, and he really was looking for a word to go with the word he already had

CUSTOMER 29: ok, ok, ok, I have a phrase

ROB: ok

CUSTOMER 29: a sentence

ROB: very good

CUSTOMER 29: would you like to join us for the Buckminster Fuller screening at the Guggenheim on Thursday night?

ROB: very nice… that's, uh, that's a lot… but it's…

CUSTOMER 29: you want a shorter phrase?

ROB: no, no, no, doesn't scare me… it's expensive I'm saying… um, a little bit, the words are one dollar

CUSTOMER 29: yeah, so that's…

ROB: …it's not terrible

CUSTOMER 29: it's like under twenty dollars

ROB: well under twenty dollars… um, no, I like that… now what's gonna happen… so we have to decide… so you like that phrase… you, you, you…

CUSTOMER 29: …yes

ROB: …you're feeling like… you're gonna… ok, comfortable with that phrase… all right, then the things we have to think about are… do we want it handwritten or printed?

CUSTOMER 29: mm-hmm

ROB: and if we want it hand-written, how?

CUSTOMER 29: mm-hmm

ROB: is it gonna be cursive? is it gonna be small? is it gonna be large? is it gonna be all caps? no caps?... lots of things to think about... is the paper going to be landscape or vertical?

CUSTOMER 29: mm-hmm

ROB: and at the end of this process it will be stamped with, um, the word shop and signed and all

CUSTOMER 29: ok

ROB: [unintelligible] printed landscape beautiful... ok... [unintelligible] ok, printed landscape all right... marker or pen?

CUSTOMER 29: marker

ROB: I think that's a really good choice

CUSTOMER 29: yeah

ROB: we'll try it with marker... if we don't like it we can throw it away and start over

CUSTOMER 29: yeah

ROB: yeah there's no, uh, the shop is very easy that way... ok the phrase... I'll get you a fresh piece of paper... here's what we'll do... I'm gonna write it because I just have to think about spacing... ok, so the phrase is...

CUSTOMER 29: would you like to join us...

ROB: would you like to join us...

CUSTOMER 29: for the Buckminster Fuller

ROB: Buckminster

CUSTOMER 29: Buckminster

ROB: Fuller... double-l ?

CUSTOMER 29: Fuller... mm-hmm... screening at the Guggenheim on Thursday night

ROB: screening at the Guggenheim... uh, i-e or e-i ?

CUSTOMER 29: i

ROB: heim... Guggenheim... e-i

CUSTOMER 29: yeah it's probably i-e... I have it spelled e-i but it's probably wrong... I'm a terrible speller

ROB: let me see... heim... I think it's i-e... we can look it up

CUSTOMER 29: ok

ROB: I'm pretty sure it's i-e... ok, at the Guggenheim

CUSTOMER 29: on Thursday night

ROB: on... and it's all caps... did we say it was gonna be all caps?

CUSTOMER 29: no

ROB: ...or no

CUSTOMER 29: no

ROB: we just said it's gonna be printed, that's right, so what do you think about the caps?... whether we want caps on Thursday Night, if we want caps we have to think about that... all right... good... ok, now let's... let me just check on Guggenheim... pretty sure I got that spelled right... it's fun to look stuff up, no? you're right... it's e-i

CUSTOMER 29: oh... hmm

ROB: see that?... don't doubt yourself... ok, it's e-i... ok, all right, so we're gonna have, um, we know that we're gonna have marker and printed... not script... not cursive... print, ok?... and initial cap or no cap or lowercase?... we could have initial cap... would be... so this would be capped

163

CUSTOMER 29: right

ROB: uh, Buckminster... we'd have to think about whether those were capped... Guggenheim Thursday Night... so... typically...

CUSTOMER 29: ...Thursday night... no, night wouldn't be capped

ROB: night wouldn't be... ok, good... so Thursday but that's our choice... we could have no caps, we can have all caps, we could have initial caps...

CUSTOMER 29: well I don't want... no, I don't want all caps... I want upper and lower case the way it might be written as a sentence or...

ROB: normally... as a sentence...

CUSTOMER 29: yeah

ROB: beautiful... ok, let's see how this goes, uh, I think we'll start about here now if it's... um...

CUSTOMER 29: I mean another thing is... I'm giving you this phrase so do... you do anything with the phrase?

ROB: no

CUSTOMER 29: you don't?

ROB: no, not unless you want me to... see I'm entirely at your disposal

CUSTOMER 29: oh

ROB: I'm just gonna copy the phrase unless you want me to do something... to edit it, to interfere with it... I could do anything

CUSTOMER 29: ok, I want you to interfere with it

ROB: ok, good

CUSTOMER 29: or edit it, or do something with it

ROB: now if I'm going to interfere, it's probably going to be major

CUSTOMER 29: oh it is

ROB: well it might be... it might be disruptive

CUSTOMER 29: it might be disruptive?

ROB: like if you want it to make sense... is that... do you want it to make sense?

CUSTOMER 29: well I want you to think about this phrase being spoken

ROB: mm-hmm

CUSTOMER 29: and listening to the voice saying this phrase

ROB: mm-hmm

CUSTOMER 29: and maybe if you're really listening to the sound of the language you might imagine that voice articulating an idea about an invitation that might be to something, ok? ...an invitation would have to be an invitation to a film... does that kind of limit it more?

ROB: mm-hmm

CUSTOMER 29: so it's someone expressing an invitation to a film... so what's important is the subject of the film thinking Buckminister... Buckminster Fuller

ROB: has to be there... mm-hmm...

CUSTOMER 29: to me, you know, it's more about phonetics and a place...

ROB: mm-hmm and it has to be the Guggenheim?... you need that information in here?

CUSTOMER 29: well Guggenheim has a particular phonetic ring to me... for me it's all about phonetics

ROB: mm-hmm

CUSTOMER 29: right

ROB: mm-hmm… mm-hmm

CUSTOMER 29: doesn't have to be the Guggenheim

ROB: oh, phonetics is… oh, very nice…

Customer 30

ROB: the longest I think was the one I just had with Sir Rodney Sir

CUSTOMER 30: oh yeah and have you had a lot of unexpected people like who you've never met?

ROB: I've had people I've never met, I have not had very many people come off the street, but I've had lots of people I've met once or never met… friend of friends

CUSTOMER 30: [inaudible] thing on their website

ROB: no that's ok with me

CUSTOMER 30: that's ok?

ROB: yeah, um, ok… everything's videotaped if that's ok with you?

CUSTOMER 30: yeah that's fine

ROB: um… and as I've been telling everyone, uh, what happens is, um, this takes care of the audio which is gonna be a book in the end

CUSTOMER 30: ok

ROB: the video… I don't know… it's gonna also be something

CUSTOMER 30: ok

ROB: ok so, um, typically what happens is that, uh, people either come in with a word or they want me to come up with a word

CUSTOMER 30: ok

ROB: um then we decide how we want it to appear which is the biggest part of our conversation... whether it's gonna be, um, on, uh, handwritten... whether it's gonna be the printer... whether it's gonna be landscape, vertical...

CUSTOMER 30: ok

ROB: all of that is, uh, takes some considering... so what are you thinking about? do you have a word in mind?

CUSTOMER 30: no

ROB: a phrase or a letter?

CUSTOMER 30: I'm totally unprepared

ROB: no, no... that's good... so if you're... we can think of something together... we can think of something that's in this room, uh, we could borrow something... we can make... originally think of something... we can look online...

CUSTOMER 30: um... let me think for a second... there have been some words that have been, um, crossing my mind namely because Luca keeps asking me about very specific descriptions of words... words that have meanings both that relate to the law like "guilty"

ROB: ah, great, that's interesting right

CUSTOMER 30: um

ROB: ...that he wants you to explain?

CUSTOMER 30: yeah like the guilty can be emo... you know emotional guilt or send you to jail

ROB: right

CUSTOMER 30: which he's very obsessed with

ROB: right, right… doesn't want to go to jail

CUSTOMER 30: um, uh, so what… once we choose the word then we talk about it or what

ROB: then we talk about how we want it to appear… whether we want it to be… most… most people have chosen… I'll tell you what the most popular choice is… the most popular choices have been, um, using the Sharpie

CUSTOMER 30: yeah?

ROB: and cursive and, um, the paper I think usually landscape although a lot of vertical too… uh… depends… the three choices really are pen, Sharpie, and computer printer

CUSTOMER 30: ok, well, I have a word since we're here

ROB: ok

CUSTOMER 30: poetic

ROB: very nice

CUSTOMER 30: in the Sharpie

ROB: Sharpie

CUSTOMER 30: landscape

ROB: poetic, um, lowercase? uppercase? printed?

CUSTOMER 30: I think, um, printed uppercase

ROB: printed… all uppercase… um, landscape or vertical?

CUSTOMER 30: landscape

ROB: now if we don't like it, by the way, we can throw it away

CUSTOMER 30: ok

ROB: ...and start over... um, landscape... all caps... prin... all caps

CUSTOMER 30: mm-hmm

ROB: all caps printed poetic... poetic-s?

CUSTOMER 30: poetic

ROB: ok... here we go

CUSTOMER 30: nice

ROB: very nice

CUSTOMER 30: yeah

ROB: you like it?

CUSTOMER 30: I do

ROB: all right good... now, as an example... I like it too... let's see what it would look like cursive

CUSTOMER 30: what was the last guy's word

ROB: he had a whole sentence... it was really interesting... it was about... it... it... and that's what the explanation was... he's writing a story and at one point he wants the character to say are you going to the Guggenheim to the Buckminster Fuller film and so that was his phrase, although I altered it to make it sound more vernacular... I just want to see for myself what this would look like, um, lowercase and script

CUSTOMER 30: it's a weird word visually, huh?

ROB: it is

CUSTOMER 30: you're really aware of the p-o-e ...

ROB: it is

CUSTOMER 30: p-o-e ...

ROB: it's... it's the p... yeah, yeah, yeah, it's true [inaudible] and you could take both of these... you can take both home because I'm just gonna throw it away

CUSTOMER 30: nice

ROB: ok so what'd you decide?... I think I like your original more but it sort of depends on what, you know, I mean these could end up in a drawer that no one really sees but you know you have...

CUSTOMER 30: ...ok

ROB: ...you know they could be... people have threatened to frame them... put them in books... all kinds of things happen, um...

CUSTOMER 30: and you don't keep one?

ROB: no I'll keep a receipt which I'll make now and you can think about, um, if there are other words [inaudible]

CUSTOMER 30: and do you... are they... do I pay you for them?

ROB: yeah, so words are one dollar

CUSTOMER 30: ok

ROB: one of these is gratis because I'm gonna throw it away... the... the letters... words are one dollar, letters are fifty cents, so Rodney just spent fifteen dollars... that's quite a lot

CUSTOMER 30: wow

ROB: yeah, that's... that's...

CUSTOMER 30: ...he got a lot of words...

ROB: ...that's one of my... that's my big... lot of words... one of... usually it's individual words... one word, maybe two words, a couple of words... thirteen words is a lot... so your word is poetic

CUSTOMER 30: one dollar is exactly what I have in my wallet

ROB: beautiful and then we have…

CUSTOMER 30: amazing… poetic, um, we'll say, uh, script… that one is gratis

ROB: ok, beautiful… would you like a folder to keep everything in so it doesn't…

CUSTOMER 30: …I would love a folder 'cause I don't have a hard bag today

DAY 11

Ledger

Left apartment at 10:48 on foot (rain was expected) and arrived at the shop around 10:57 AM. Set-up from 11:00-11:10. Immediately following set-up, I received my first 2 customers who came in together. This will prove to be the busiest day of Rob's Word Shop as I was continually busy from 11:10 AM until closing at 2 PM and then another 30 minutes of overtime.

Customer 31 requested that I assist him in his choice of a phrase. After considerable discussion about his new project, we decided upon the phrase: all that's left. Total sale: $3.00.

Customer 32 also requested my assistance. In this case, we enjoyed a lively conversation about a famously disputed umpiring call in the 1985 baseball World Series between the St. Louis Cardinals and the Kansas City Royals—a call that went the Royals' way and heavily influenced the outcome of the 1985 World Series. The phrase that we decided upon together was: I'M STILLIN'. Total sale: $2.00.

Customer 33 arrived around 11:30 and patiently waited for Customers 31 and 32 to finish their business. When it was her turn, Customers 31 and 32 stayed on to assist Customer 33 in her choosing. Customer 33 purchased 7 words, on 5 separate sheets of paper (1 purchase was a phrase). There was a collaborative discussion between myself, Customer 33, and Customers 31 and 32 for each of her words/phrases; the results were:

> Balslamic
> Galvanic
> Azurious
> Seabed
> Lights, for sure

Total sale for Customer 33 was $7.00.

Customer 34 arrived around 12:30 and purchased 4 words on 4 separate sheets of paper. The words were: BIRD / WILL / SING / A. Total sale: $4.00.

Customer 35 also arrived around 12:15 when several other customers arrived. He purchased 1 word: Their. This word was related to a 1960s comedy skit about bartering words. Additionally, as a gift from the shop to his family, I scribed the following phrase gratis: Where are you?
Total sale: $1.00.

At this point, I took inventory of my paper supply because I had a few new customers who had large orders. I realized that I was about to run out of paper, so Customer 35 graciously offered to watch the shop while I ran to the stationary store 3 blocks away. I was gone for 8 minutes.

Customer 36 arrived with a list of 19 letters, words, and phrases to be purchased. They were:

> PORTLAND
> ICELAND
> HEATH
> BATMAN
> WITCHYPOO
> MUDKIP
> PANDA
> BONDI
> VIRUS
> READING
> EQUALS (gratis)
> DISTRACTION
> PONG
> SONY
> SQUARE ENIX
> MARIJUANA
> DREAMWORKS
> ILYY
> Tl;dr

Total sale: $18.00 (1 word gratis for purchasing over $10).

Customer 37, who had arrived with Customer 36, purchased 2 words: Committee and Ampersand. The latter was purchased as a series of letters from a stencil set. Total sale: $2.00.

Customer 38, who had been waiting patiently, purchased the following:

> W/
> Tangentially Judicious
> Landmine
> Through (across 2 sheets of paper)

Total sale: $4.50

The computer ran out of power halfway through Customer 38's transaction. Customer 39, who entered with customer 38, ordered the following words and phrases but they were not recorded by the video:

> SPARKLE
> DRESS CIRCLE
> LASHES
> PEANUT
> CHARITY
> ORVIL PYM
> GALLEYS
> DUPLICITIOUS
> DARLING
> DARLING
> CRISP
> TUBULAR (gratis)

Total sale: $13.00

Customer 40 arrived around 1:45. We had agreed to a barter arrangement beforehand—he exchanged 2 CDs from his band for the following purchase: approximately 60 periods and algae & tentacles.

Total sale: $0 (barter exchange).

Customer 41 purchased 4 words (plus 1 gratis):

> *AJaR*
> *SINK SYNC ("sync" was gratis because it was suggested by the other customers that it is nearly the same word)*
> *ROBERT*
> *FITTERMAN*

ROBERT and FITTERMAN were written in script as a signature; Customer 41 wanted the words written inside of a book titled "Notes On Conceptualisms."

Total sale: $4.00

After these final orders were completed, I packed up the tools of the shop (stamps, receipts books, markers, etc.), disconnected the printer, and removed the signage. I deposited a large tip at the café and left the shop at 3:10 PM.

Total for the day: $58.50.

Rob's Word Shop was officially closed at 2:25 PM.

Walked home with printer and the tools of the shop. Listened to a phone message on the walk home from a potential customer asking if the store had already been closed—in the hopes that the store was still open, he recited a list of letters for a phone order. I called him back at 3:20 PM and left a message explaining that the shop was already closed.

Customer 31 (with Customers 32, 33)

ROB: ok, so who's ready who wants to begin?

CUSTOMER 31: well I'll start [unintelligible]… I don't have words chosen…

ROB: ok…

CUSTOMER 31: …but I'm in the middle of trying to start a poem I've had in mind for some time

ROB: ok

CUSTOMER 31: and I'm having a little trouble getting started

ROB: mm-hmm

CUSTOMER 31: um, so I think I'd like some language that could become axiomatic or galvanic inside that poem… that can magnetize some other language, some other tropes

ROB: mm-hmm

CUSTOMER 31: um… that can help me get that made

ROB: mm-hmm

CUSTOMER 31: that's really what I need to do

ROB: mm-hmm

CUSTOMER 31: because I'm almost done with my book… I've got to have it done by the end of September to get it to the, uh, to the person who's gonna print it and I just I wanna finish this manuscript desperately

ROB: mm-hmm

CUSTOMER 31: um… so I would like some language for that

ROB: mm-hmm

CUSTOMER 31: a couple of words even

ROB: mm-hmm

CUSTOMER 31: and the poem that I have in mind is about... it's funny when I thought she said her daughter's name was Willow... this is going to be even more important... but the poem is about Willow Rosenberg's resurrection spell that brings Buffy back from the dead

ROB: mm-hmm

CUSTOMER 31: a very powerful sort of image-system in the program

ROB: mm-hmm

CUSTOMER 31: I mean it's a very powerful sort of narrative

ROB: mm-hmm

CUSTOMER 31: about the familial grief, although this is a family that's constituted by friends essentially... I mean one of the interesting things that happens on the show is that family members die or their irreality becomes made manifest and all that's left is the... are these friends, um...

CUSTOMER 33: ...thank God

CUSTOMER 31: I know, and they kind of constitute as family and this is... this...

CUSTOMER 32: well this is like the story of high school anyway

CUSTOMER 31: yeah right

CUSTOMER 32: especially [unintelligible] subculture in high school

CUSTOMER 31: right, right, right, um... and this is the major trope in the book and my own book… anyway, um, so, so I'm sorry I know you're in the middle of watching it… I'm giving some things away

CUSTOMER 32: no, yeah, you really spoiled things for me

CUSTOMER 31: I know

CUSTOMER 32: and um…

CUSTOMER 31: …you're welcome

CUSTOMER 32: this is probably the last time we hang out

CUSTOMER 31: I was gonna say this is it for us, isn't it?… well… I think my word's gonna be au revoir right? I have time to think about this, so don't… you didn't charge me for that did you?

ROB: no, yeah, so far the meter is not running

CUSTOMER 31: right

CUSTOMER 32: ok, all right

CUSTOMER 31: um… first of all, it was worth it to loose you as a friend… I'm gonna get two dollars worth of fucking words here

CUSTOMER 32: yeah, it's true, you know, fair enough

CUSTOMER 31: um… now… so that's what I've got

ROB: ok it's interesting and you're thinking about a phrase that's gonna…

CUSTOMER 31: or even a word or two that become magnetic you know

ROB: mm-hmm… mm-hmm…

CUSTOMER 31: that could draw the language towards it

ROB: mm-hmm, mm-hmm, mm-hmm, and are you thinking about a word or phrase that is, um, uh… innocuous or that has some lights around it?

CUSTOMER 31: lights for sure

ROB: lights for sure

CUSTOMER 31: yeah

ROB: ok good

CUSTOMER 31: over-saturated

ROB: over-saturated

CUSTOMER 31: as opposed to prosaic, yeah

ROB: mm-hmm, mm-hmm, that's exactly what I was wondering… ok, good… um…

CUSTOMER 31: I definitely want the Sharpie, by the way

ROB: of course, um, ok and anything that has that… that you had on your mind already… that we could work with? or you want me to…

CUSTOMER 31: I'd like you to choose it

ROB: …throw some things up

CUSTOMER 31: yeah, yeah

ROB: first word that came to mind when you said extravagant in this case was opulence

CUSTOMER 31: uh-huh, mm-hmm

ROB: …because I like the gothic… it has this…

CUSTOMER 31: sure…

ROB: …kind of like gothic thing I like… but I like… and… and when you didn't… when a… when I wasn't sure you wanted something so grand… I like the repetition of this idea… of all that's left… which I'm just quoting you when you said "all that's left" are these friends

CUSTOMER 31: I like that though

ROB: because the all…

CUSTOMER 31: …I do like that

ROB: all that's left is, um, you know… you know a nice beginning

CUSTOMER 31: sure

ROB: …and… you know, and it br… I like the way you could kinda cast this whole apocalyptic…

CUSTOMER 31: I do like that, mm-hmm, and that's… mm-hmm… and that's in the tenor… that's in the tenor of the poem for sure… I've used opulence twice in the manuscript already so probably not again

ROB: you've used opulence twice? wow!

CUSTOMER 33: [inaudible] you know that?

CUSTOMER 31: yeah

ROB: you might have to name…

CUSTOMER 31: 'cause I really…

ROB: …the damn thing that

CUSTOMER 31: I know

CUSTOMER 32: right

CUSTOMER 31: I just really like the word, so I'm very sensitive to overusing words

CUSTOMER 33: yeah

CUSTOMER 31: I'm really attracted to…

CUSTOMER 33: now I'm curious about what other words you used more than once

CUSTOMER 31: I know I have to think about that

ROB: you know the... the more I'm thinking in my mind of all that's left there's something about it that is slightly Edwardian...

CUSTOMER 31: uh huh

ROB: ...and even though it is a very simple phrase too

CUSTOMER 31: yeah

ROB: ...something kind of potentially...

CUSTOMER 31: ...it is really good actually

CUSTOMER 32: but there is also, of course, a great spirit of doom around it because its messianic... it's like the time that remains or something

CUSTOMER 31: sure exactly

CUSTOMER 32: there is a sort of...

CUSTOMER 31: right

CUSTOMER 32: eschatological...

ROB: right

CUSTOMER 31: as there should be... end of the world for Buffy

ROB: right

CUSTOMER 31: she's the mess... messianic figure I mean here she is...

CUSTOMER 32: don't... please don't say anymore

CUSTOMER 31: yeah, yeah, you know what's up man

ROB: should we try that with a marker?

CUSTOMER 31: yeah

ROB: ...or should we keep thinking

CUSTOMER 31: no I want that

ROB: all right

CUSTOMER 31: that's right

ROB: um... do we like it, uh, you want... do you want to make decisions about how it's gonna look? do you want me to make decisions?

CUSTOMER 31: um... I think I would actually... I would like it pretty big

ROB: pretty big

CUSTOMER 31: across the middle of the page

ROB: landscape?

CUSTOMER 31: so I can... so I can have it on my wall

ROB: landscape big across the page?

CUSTOMER 31: yeah

ROB: script?

CUSTOMER 31: uh...

ROB: ...or print?

CUSTOMER 31: print

ROB: I'm gonna... I'm gonna, uh, give you both... ok, well, you can throw this one away... you're not getting charged for it

CUSTOMER 31: uh-huh

ROB: and then this one... and I put the stamp on the front usually... I put the stamp on the front but I always ask... you could have the stamp on the back... you could have no stamp at all

CUSTOMER 31: uh...

ROB: ...that's up to you... you could have it in the middle... you could... you... your...

CUSTOMER 31: I think no stamp

ROB: no stamp?

CUSTOMER 31: mm-hmm

ROB: all right I'm not offended... ok, now you get a receipt and, uh, you'll get your stamp there

CUSTOMER 31: right

ROB: so... um...

CUSTOMER 32: do you take American Express?

ROB: I'm sorry, no... cash only

CUSTOMER 32: ok, that's fine

Customer 32 (with Customers 31, 33)

CUSTOMER 32: I've had a lot of a lot of ideas for what we could talk about here but since we have... our time is short...

ROB: no, no...

CUSTOMER 32: I, well...

ROB: you know, but I... ee... ee... you've been soul searching... I think is, uh, yeah...

CUSTOMER 32: what I've been thinking about Rob is...

ROB: …yeah

CUSTOMER 32: …uh, our relationship

ROB: yeah

CUSTOMER 32: and I think that for the most part we get along very, very well

ROB: yes, indeed

CUSTOMER 32: um… I also think that there's one… there is a point of contention between us that… not just you and I but with many people… um… that's never been resolved and I think I… I'm hoping we can resolve it through language today, um, and it's about the 1985 World Series

ROB: yes

CUSTOMER 32: so I would… I think… I think that there was a call made in the eighth inning of game six that you believe was made in error

ROB: I… who doesn't?

CUSTOMER 32: well I believe that it was made correctly and so I was wondering how you could… do you have any ideas about how we could solve this problem so we can move forward?

CUSTOMER 31: [inaudible]

CUSTOMER 32: …in complete agreement?

ROB: now, see, this is very complicated in many interesting ways

CUSTOMER 32: it's a lyric question

ROB: what we have to investigate, I think, in this lyric question is resolution itself

CUSTOMER 32: mmm…

ROB: can we live without the resolution that's…

CUSTOMER 32: …right…

ROB: …that's the hard…

CUSTOMER 32: …what we do have… we do have, of course, we have history

ROB: yes

CUSTOMER 32: somebody was in charge… a figure of authority made a decision

ROB: that's right

CUSTOMER 32: that, um, had effects in the real world

ROB: that's right

CUSTOMER 32: um…

ROB: and, uh, right or wrong it's…

CUSTOMER 32: …right…

ROB: …a decision

CUSTOMER 32: right… right… so we can be critical of history but so we [unitelligible] negotiate with the material facts of history, you know, where the spoils went

ROB: right… now, Denninger… right? …Denninger

CUSTOMER 31: right… I think that's right

CUSTOMER 32: Denk… Denkinger

ROB: Denkinger… first name John maybe

CUSTOMER 32: Don

CUSTOMER 33: it's already falling apart… they haven't even

[inaudible]…

ROB: Don?

CUSTOMER 32: Don

ROB: Don

CUSTOMER 32: Don Denkinger

ROB: Don Denkinger

CUSTOMER 32: I think… right… I don't have my iPhone with me

ROB: I think that's right… Don is definitely right… well, the first… well… well, ok, this is very good… so there's a lot to think about here… you know I have a poem written about that very moment

CUSTOMER 32: I did not know that

ROB: in my youth

CUSTOMER 32: uh-huh

ROB: it was written in 1985

CUSTOMER 32: mm-hmm

ROB: right after he called "the call"

CUSTOMER 32: "the call"

ROB: yeah

CUSTOMER 32: as it's known in parlance

CUSTOMER 31: mm-hmm

ROB: right… right… um, but I can't… I don't remember well enough to recall any of it

CUSTOMER 32: it must have been a very angry poem given…

ROB: nah... it was about the ridiculousness of the... the... that... that it was still hurtful

CUSTOMER 32: all right... the absurdity of the trauma

ROB: yeah

CUSTOMER 32: yeah

ROB: and that word still was central

CUSTOMER 32: uh-huh

ROB: [inaudible] continuing...

CUSTOMER 32: that might be a candidate for our word

ROB: right

CUSTOMER 32: as a way for you to heal

ROB: mm-hmm... still just as by itself, a pretty powerful word

CUSTOMER 32: yeah pretty much... what I mean...

ROB: ...pretty interesting word

CUSTOMER 32: yeah

ROB: yeah, um, so on the... the... so that's very nice—let me take some notes here, yeah, still is very nice... it's funny because someone came in... they wanted a noun and verb and came up with, uh, a word that was both a noun and a verb... we had a lot of options

CUSTOMER 32: mm-hmm... noun and adjective

ROB: noun and adjective and...

CUSTOMER 32: ...adverb

ROB: you can't have a...

CUSTOMER 32: ...I'm still...

ROB: right you can't still... you can't be stillin'

CUSTOMER 32: yeah, you can't be stillin'

CUSTOMER 31: I'm stillin'

CUSTOMER 32: I'm stillin'... actually that's...

CUSTOMER 31: ...I know

ROB: that could be a possibility too

CUSTOMER 32: I'm stillin'

ROB: still I'm stillin'

CUSTOMER 31: yeah

CUSTOMER 32: I'm stillin'

CUSTOMER 31: but stillin' as a contraction

CUSTOMER 32: stillin' with an apostrophe

CUSTOMER 31: yeah

CUSTOMER 32: right

ROB: yeah

CUSTOMER 31: yeah

CUSTOMER 31: as a kind of innovation in hip hop vernacular

CUSTOMER 32: yeah, yeah

ROB: with, uh, wi... it could be with or without... with... uh with apostrophe

CUSTOMER 33: yeah

CUSTOMER 32: and you know, also, you know you have the words I'm still in...

CUSTOMER 31: I know...

CUSTOMER 32: which is, um, exactly the situation for the Kansas City Royals... they're still in the record book as the 19...

ROB: ...right...

CUSTOMER 32: ...1985 World Series Champions

CUSTOMER 31: right, yeah

CUSTOMER 33: and you're still in your argument

CUSTOMER 32: until this is... until the transaction

CUSTOMER 33: yeah, but Rob's not buying your argument

CUSTOMER 32: oh, right

ROB: but I could be stillin'

CUSTOMER 31: uh-huh

CUSTOMER 32: yeah, right, right, it also sort of... I think we're leaning really heavily here... but it's also like you can hear the words I'm stealin'

CUSTOMER 31: stealin' ...that's what I got too

CUSTOMER 32: like I've stolen the World Series...

CUSTOMER 31: ...yeah yeah

CUSTOMER 32: ...away from the Cardinals

CUSTOMER 31: I know

ROB: right, right, right

CUSTOMER 31: I hear that... that's what I heard as well

CUSTOMER 32: I think... I think this is maybe a go, Rob

ROB: all right good should we bother with the, uh, seeing what...

CUSTOMER 32: why don't I just purchase this from you, Rob, and...

ROB: ...forget about the rest of it?

CUSTOMER 32: [unintelligible] other customers waiting and we... we should...

CUSTOMER 33: oh yeah but I'm [inaudible]...

ROB: all right, good, um... and you don't need to... you don't need another version?

CUSTOMER 32: I think I'm ok with this

ROB: look at that... no more buyer's remorse!

CUSTOMER 32: I know

ROB: maybe you're cured

CUSTOMER 32: well, see, 'cause if you had written... here's the problem... if you do make another one, I will be racked with such indecision and I may never leave

CUSTOMER 33: yeah

CUSTOMER 32: so...

ROB: that's... that could be a problem... although as much as I love your company, you probably don't want to spend the rest of your life here... ok, good, so two words... contractions are, uh...

CUSTOMER 32: ...yeah, I think... so I... do you think I can get a folder?

ROB: a folder?

CUSTOMER 32: yeah

ROB: that was gonna be my next question... folder?

CUSTOMER 33: Rob, has anyone brought back their word?

ROB: no, I've had no...

CUSTOMER 31: ...no returns?

ROB: I... I'm open to returns or exchanges

CUSTOMER 33: yeah...

ROB: and I haven't had any, um...

CUSTOMER 31: layaway?

ROB: I haven't had any layaway... I mean I have had a few... um... I have some delinquent...

CUSTOMER 33: yeah?

CUSTOMER 32: oh

ROB: ...uh, orders, you know...

CUSTOMER 32: how do you plan on taking care of that?

ROB: I don't know... a collection agency maybe...

CUSTOMER 32: yeah

ROB: maybe I'll get you on that... I... I don't know

CUSTOMER 32: to do collection? I wear pink pants... I don't know if I'm terribly imposing... you owe Rob Fitterman money!

CUSTOMER 31: sure

CUSTOMER 32: it's like puh-shhh

CUSTOMER 31: yeah, sure

CUSTOMER 32: yeah, sure

Customer 33 (with Customers 31, 32)

ROB: you can have seedbed instead of seabed if you prefer

CUSTOMER 33: what about both of them on the same page, even though I love that you could just…

ROB: …I think… I think you need to start over

CUSTOMER 33: what do you guys think about both of them on the same page?

CUSTOMER 33: bed seedbed

ROB: I think you're gonna ruin it having both on… it's gonna be too…

CUSTOMER 33: …too much?

ROB: too much

CUSTOMER 33: it's too…

CUSTOMER 31: [inaudible] it's a magical…

CUSTOMER 33: yeah

CUSTOMER 31: …word that combines a surface we're totally habituated to… our bed

CUSTOMER 33: yeah…

CUSTOMER 31: …to one that's like exotic and far away

CUSTOMER 33: oh that's such a nice way of describing it

CUSTOMER 31: I think… I think that's more uncanny…

CUSTOMER 33: that's such a nice way of describing it… I wish I could have that whole fairytale you just told trailing underneath my word, right?… it's really nice… ok, so we got two…

ROB: yeah... ok, good, so... um, what's next? ...so this is two year old... this is three year old... um

CUSTOMER 31: that'll be really funny [inaudible]

ROB: oh all right... I thought that because her first is gone already... but you're gonna make up for it and give her that for her first birthday... great, ok, good so then this is three... we've gotta redo the numbers... so what do you want for four?

CUSTOMER 33: I don't know

ROB: you have galvanic

CUSTOMER 33: I love galvanic

ROB: let's go with galvanic

CUSTOMER 33: but I feel like you... yeah, all right...

ROB: now do you want galvanic in the same script or you want me... start to shake it up... galvanic might look good all caps... it's got a, you know, let's try it... let's see what it looks like...

CUSTOMER 33: so when we're done will you tell me some of the different words that moms have bought for their kids

ROB: you can look on the blog, it's...

CUSTOMER 33: ...so you're not telling?...

ROB: no I'll tell you, but they're all on the blog

CUSTOMER 33: Kim got some words for, um, Coco right?

ROB: selfhood

CUSTOMER 33: selfhood?

CUSTOMER 31: that is great, yeah

CUSTOMER 33: yeah beautiful

ROB: and then Judah's mom for Ike got I ... an I a K and an E on three separate pages... one I, one K, and one E.

CUSTOMER 33: uh-huh

ROB: ...and had each individual one framed for his birthday

CUSTOMER 33: that's nice

ROB: yeah which he apparently liked a lot and he's...

CUSTOMER 33: ...he did?...

ROB: ...sixteen... he doesn't like anything

CUSTOMER 33: yeah great and so then...

ROB: yeah, now, seabed is a lighter... is that... do you like it? it's, uh, it's, uh, thinner... I... I could redo that

CUSTOMER 33: no it's ok... that's such a beautiful word

ROB: you had me working... you got your money's worth

CUSTOMER 33: I'm really gonna leave a satisfied customer

Customer 34 (with Customers 35, 36, 37, 38)

ROB: so the way this goes generally is you... do you have words in mind?

CUSTOMER 34: I do but...

ROB: ...all right, good

CUSTOMER 34: I have words in mind

ROB: great now, uh, most of the time there are three tools... there's a Sharpie, a pen, or a printer... um, I don't use the... don't use the printer a lot, um, most people choose a Sharpie but it's entirely up to you, then we decide, like, what it's going to look like on the page

CUSTOMER 34: ok

ROB: so that... that's... that's sort of everything

CUSTOMER 34: that sounds great

ROB: ok

CUSTOMER 34: I'm inclined to the pen

ROB: ok

CUSTOMER 34: yeah

ROB: that's great, we'll work with the pen... if you don't like it we can...

CUSTOMER 35: ...it's mightier than the sword

CUSTOMER 34: and perhaps than the Sharpie

CUSTOMER 36: no the Sharpie's mightier

ROB: ...and if we don't like it, we'll move on... ok? good? what are you thinking about?

CUSTOMER 34: well I have, um, four words

ROB: yeah

CUSTOMER 34: and it's a phrase but I think I should shop in order of words and not just the phrase

ROB: ok

CUSTOMER 34: so my first word is will

ROB: so they're gonna go on separate pieces of paper

CUSTOMER 34: yeah, yeah

ROB: ok now... so let's give it... give... give us a sense of what this is gonna look like... separate pieces of paper um...

CUSTOMER 35: do you have samples?

ROB: yep we'll do samples... um, were you thinking landscape or vertical, horizontal or vertical... I mean the page...

CUSTOMER 34: vertical

ROB: vertical, ok, good... you thinking, um, script or print? cursive or print?

CUSTOMER 34: print

ROB: print

CUSTOMER 34: yeah

ROB: big or small?

CUSTOMER 34: big

ROB: big, ok, on... so with pen... let's give a sample just so you can see

CUSTOMER 34: ok

ROB: so

CUSTOMER 34: ...know what I'm getting into right?

ROB: yeah you should know what you're getting into... so, with pen it's gonna look like that... it looks like... right? print?

CUSTOMER 34: yeah

ROB: with the all caps

CUSTOMER 34: yeah that's good

ROB: ok and with...

CUSTOMER 34: [inaudible]

CUSTOMER 35 [OFF]: is that like a high school?

ROB: I think...

CUSTOMER 34: I changed my mind

ROB: I don't blame you... that's what happens

CUSTOMER 35 [OFF]: they've been in there since I've been here

ROB: ok, so will is the first...

CUSTOMER 34: will

ROB: ok, let's... uh... take this paper off so it doesn't bleed through

CUSTOMER 37 [OFF]: yeah we have lived here for like five or six years

CUSTOMER 35: [inaudible]

CUSTOMER 37: well we've been doing to...

ROB: ...will

CUSTOMER 34: will

ROB: very good... next?

CUSTOMER 35 [OFF]: I don't live here

CUSTOMER 34: bird

CUSTOMER 37 [OFF]: oh, ok, where are you?

ROB: ...bird

CUSTOMER 34: bird

ROB: ok

CUSTOMER 37 [OFF]: I thought you lived here... maybe you did... [inaudible]

ROB: same general?…

CUSTOMER 34: same general size and [inaudible]

CUSTOMER 37 [OFF]: so where are you living?

CUSTOMER 35 [OFF]: in the Hudson Valley

CUSTOMER 37 [OFF]: sorry?

CUSTOMER 35 [OFF]: in the Hudson Valley

CUSTOMER 37 [OFF]: ok

ROB: …bird

CUSTOMER 34: bird… great, that's great

ROB: all right next?

CUSTOMER 34: and then I have, um…

CUSTOMER 37 [OFF]: I'm sorry what did you just say?

CUSTOMER 34: sing… sing…

ROB: sing… sing?

CUSTOMER 34: and then the last one is, uh, a… a…

ROB: a

CUSTOMER 35: you're making it easy on him

CUSTOMER 34: I am? well, you know, small words are strong like will… that's a strong word… a lot of things can happen in will

CUSTOMER 37: mm-hmm

ROB: now typically…

CUSTOMER 35: you're not challenging his orthographic skill maybe

CUSTOMER 36: do you do Chinese, Rob?

ROB: no, but, uh, I'm open to anything... ok, now typically I stamp them on the front

CUSTOMER 34: yes

ROB: but if you don't want that we can do it on the back

CUSTOMER 34: I like this frontal stamp

ROB: yeah

CUSTOMER 34: that seems very certified

ROB: ok... they're beautiful

CUSTOMER 34: wow, what's the stamp?

ROB: yep, ok, there's the stamp

CUSTOMER 34: Rob's Word Shop... oh, very nice

ROB: ok, there's page one

CUSTOMER 34: thank you... wow, certified

CUSTOMER 35: certified... certified word official

CUSTOMER 34: can people buy multiple?... like the same people buy the same... different people buy the same word?

ROB: yeah, the... my inventory is infinite

CUSTOMER 34: infinite!... I see

ROB: yeah so if somebody, in fact, somebody wanted to, to, uh, create... he manipulated the market... really created, uh, the most popular item

CUSTOMER 34: oh

ROB: so that if people came in and said what's your most... your best selling item... so my best selling item is the letter S

CUSTOMER 34: really?

ROB: because someone came in and bought a lot of letter S's

CUSTOMER 34: ah

ROB: to manipulate the market

CUSTOMER 35: oh

CUSTOMER 36: uh-huh

CUSTOMER 34: I see

CUSTOMER 37: was that James?

ROB: no, but James bought the first S... it was Zultanski who bought the other S's

CUSTOMER 37: oh yeah

CUSTOMER 34: oh my God... wow!

ROB: ok?

CUSTOMER 34: wow!

ROB: these... these are very nice... now would you like a folder to keep them in?

CUSTOMER 34: oh that would be so...

ROB: ...or you can have an envelope if you don't want a big thing

CUSTOMER 34: I'll have an envelope

ROB: ok then you have to fold it

CUSTOMER 34: uh... that's not good... I'll have a folder

ROB: yeah, see

CUSTOMER 36: yeah

ROB: after being in business for awhile...

CUSTOMER 36: they're works of art

CUSTOMER 34: yeah, I can't have that?

ROB: [inaudible]

CUSTOMER 35: hey, look at that

CUSTOMER 34: wow

ROB: that's Tim's photograph

CUSTOMER 34: oh

CUSTOMER 36: oh

CUSTOMER 37: oh

CUSTOMER 35: oh

CUSTOMER 36: very nice

CUSTOMER 35: [inaudible]

ROB: yep

CUSTOMER 35: yep

CUSTOMER 34: wow... then... I, then, I have to settle up with you

ROB: yeah I gotta give you a receipt

CUSTOMER 34: ok

ROB: so receipt's my favorite part... so we have one word which was...

CUSTOMER 34: will

ROB: start with a and a word that was will [unintelligible] and a word that was sing and a word that was bird

CUSTOMER 34: yes

ROB: beautiful words

CUSTOMER 34: oh, thank you

ROB: a bird will sing is one possibility

CUSTOMER 34: that is a possibility

ROB: but that's not the only one

CUSTOMER 34: ...in the balance [inaudible]

ROB: a bird will sing

CUSTOMER 34: not a bird sings but a bird will sing

CUSTOMER 35: "...and your bird can sing"

CUSTOMER 34: yes

ROB: "and your bird can sing"

CUSTOMER 36: The Beatles' song?

ROB: that's such a great song

CUSTOMER 34: but it's a new song and it might be the title track and I'm not gonna know...

CUSTOMER 37 [OFF]: ...I just had coffee

ROB: wow...

CUSTOMER 35: it's an early LSD song

CUSTOMER 34: so I needed... I needed to have this...

CUSTOMER 37: ok...

ROB: is that true? ok...

CUSTOMER 35: it has backwards guitar

ROB: yeah?

CUSTOMER 35: I think so

CUSTOMER 34: yeah, it looks fantastic [inaudible]—gorgeous!

ROB: there you are... you're happy?

CUSTOMER 34: I'm very happy

ROB: better than Daffy's right?

CUSTOMER 34: oh yeah... Daffy's is... you can't find anything... I was there for a full hour... here with you in five minutes

ROB: and leave...

CUSTOMER 34: got exactly what I wanted

ROB: got what you wanted... you're happy, I'm happy...

CUSTOMER 34: so what do I owe you?

ROB: four dollars

CUSTOMER 34: four dollars

ROB: I might even have, um...

CUSTOMER 34: I'll give you a twenty dollars... how's that sound?

CUSTOMER 35: what about sales tax?

CUSTOMER 34: what did I give you?

ROB: ...no tax

CUSTOMER 34: I gave you three dollars in quarters

ROB: gave me three dollars in quarters

CUSTOMER 34: ok

CUSTOMER 35: it's all on tape that you didn't charge tax for this

ROB: I don't charge tax because...

CUSTOMER 34: ...three dollars...

ROB: I'm involved in the non-profit organization of the Bowery Poetry Club

CUSTOMER 35: ah

CUSTOMER 34: oh, I see, no tax on birds

ROB: I was going to...

CUSTOMER 35: ...you're videotaping?

ROB: yeah... yep... I was gonna do a, uh, [unintelligible] was my first choice... just sit there by myself... uh, but then I'd have to pay even more... lose more money than I'm already losing

CUSTOMER 34: ok here you go

ROB: beautiful

CUSTOMER 34: voila!

ROB: thank you

CUSTOMER 34: thank you... it's been a pleasure shopping with you

ROB: good... you had a good shopping experience?

CUSTOMER 34: very good

ROB: good

CUSTOMER 34: probably the best shopping experience I've had in a while

ROB: oh, I'm so happy to hear that... very good...

CUSTOMER 36: it's the service really that makes the difference

CUSTOMER 34: yeah

CUSTOMER 36: yeah

CUSTOMER 34: all of it

CUSTOMER 36: really?

CUSTOMER 34: anything you want

Customer 35 (with Customers 36, 37)

ROB: oh, we'll just keep this... we'll keep the film going ok? ...you already know what your word is and everything?

CUSTOMER 35: yeah

ROB: all right and you want a half sheet

CUSTOMER 35: mine is an homage to that Coyle and Sharpe routine I sent you

ROB: oh yeah

CUSTOMER 35: "The Word Trade", you know, Coyle and Sharpe...

CUSTOMER 36: yeah?

CUSTOMER 35: you know "The Word Trade"?

CUSTOMER 36: no I don't know that

ROB: that was great

CUSTOMER 35: they go up to a guy in the street and they're saying: "excuse me sir, um, we're involved in a project of word trade we would like to trade a nonmaterial object word for a material object... what is that you're carrying?... ah this is a cake"

ROB: cake?

CUSTOMER 35: "my cohorts and I at work are going to consume it… we'd like to offer you a word in exchange for that cake… we were thinking the possessive pronoun *their* and the guy is like… well, I already have use of *their*… full use any time of the day or night."

CUSTOMER 36: oh that's great

CUSTOMER 35: it's really funny

ROB: and when was that done?

CUSTOMER 35: this is mid-60s… they did… they were… they were… they were guys who did that… went out and did these street routines with that… they recorded… they're brilliant… they're really fabulous… so I would like the possessive pronoun their in a Sharpie, all in caps

ROB: not… not script? …all in caps?

CUSTOMER 35: yeah

ROB: and, um, uh, middle of the page?

CUSTOMER 35: yeah, you're gonna have to fit this on their maybe

ROB: mm-hmm… yep

CUSTOMER 35: might want to plan for that

ROB: so we're going up here, um, all caps did you say?… right… oh that's beautiful on their

CUSTOMER 35: what about, um…

ROB: all caps or initial?

CUSTOMER 35: what about all caps but with an italic slant?

ROB: all caps in an italic slant… I'll try it.

CUSTOMER 36 [OFF]: what is that?

CUSTOMER 35: it's a rock

ROB: are you happy with that?

CUSTOMER 35: I like it a lot... beautiful

CUSTOMER 36 [OFF]: are they from upstate?

CUSTOMER 35: yeah I found them in a stream yesterday

CUSTOMER 36: that looks nice... yeah I think I'm gonna go with that

CUSTOMER 37: I like the layout of the half sheet

CUSTOMER 36: I do too

CUSTOMER 37: and that up at the top

CUSTOMER 35: I'm always thinking

ROB: always thinking... that's my boy... um, folder or envelope?

CUSTOMER 35: here's what I'm kinda wondering... I'm wondering if it's possible to have that mailed to me since I don't live in this town and I'm gonna be schlepping around and... can you... can you mail these to me?

ROB: yes

CUSTOMER 35: ...so I don't ruin it...

ROB: yes

CUSTOMER 35: ...on my way around town...

Customer 36 (with Customers 35, 37, 38)

ROB: there we go

CUSTOMER 36: ok

CUSTOMER 37: I like this poetry

ROB: ok, first word

CUSTOMER 36: the first word is portland

ROB: portland?

CUSTOMER 36: yes

ROB: um… horizontal or vertical?

CUSTOMER 36: horizontal please

ROB: and we were talking… the first few are…

CUSTOMER 36: um

ROB: …cursive?

CUSTOMER 36: script yeah

ROB: initial cap?

CUSTOMER 36: yes please

ROB: portland… it's a beautiful word

CUSTOMER 36: so let's do all these in this style

ROB: ok

CUSTOMER 37: I like that script

CUSTOMER 36: yeah that's a nice… that's a nice script, isn't it?… all right… so the next one is the last name of a Chinese performance artist or pop artist Bandi, b-a-n-d-i ... perfect

ROB: bandi... nice

CUSTOMER 36: yeah and then virus... perfect I like that... the u looks a little worried

ROB: another fortunate accident... all righty...

CUSTOMER 36: and, uh, reading

ROB: reading

CUSTOMER 36: yeah... very nice

CUSTOMER 37: do you have a stapler?

ROB: I don't... I have had no... uh...

CUSTOMER 37: ...need...

ROB: ...requests for one... I have tape

CUSTOMER 37: I want to know how to, um, make them stay together

ROB: we could tape them onto a piece of paper

CUSTOMER 36: yeah... equals

ROB: equals?

CUSTOMER 36: yeah the actual word

ROB: the actual word

CUSTOMER 37: gluestick? oh no...

ROB: this guy's got a tall order sorry

CUSTOMER 36: oh yeah

CUSTOMER 38 [OFF]: it's ok we don't mind as long as you are willing to go past...

ROB: oh yeah, I'm going way past today...

CUSTOMER 38: ok, ok

CUSTOMER 36: distraction

ROB [OFF]: you in a rush?

CUSTOMER 38 [OFF]: no

ROB: all right good

CUSTOMER 37: I am... you should just be like the store is closing

CUSTOMER 36: distraction

ROB: distraction

CUSTOMER 36: mm-hmm

ROB: all righty

CUSTOMER 36: pong like the game

ROB: p-a-w-n

CUSTOMER 36: p-o-n-g

ROB: oh... pong... same way that these others...?

CUSTOMER 36: yeah let's stick with this style... I like this style

ROB: pong

CUSTOMER 36: nice

ROB: beautiful

CUSTOMER 35: sun's comin' out

CUSTOMER 36: sony

ROB: what is it?

CUSTOMER 36: sony

ROB: sony

CUSTOMER 35: registered trademark

CUSTOMER 36: uh no... I mean it is but you don't have to put that part...

CUSTOMER 37: [inaudible]

CUSTOMER 36: eh? I don't know... what do you think?... that's not a bad idea

ROB: that one came out with more bold... what...

CUSTOMER 35: it would be nice with a little red trademark

CUSTOMER 36: yeah put the trademark in, why not?

CUSTOMER 37: r

CUSTOMER 36: is that what is it... tm?

CUSTOMER 35: r

CUSTOMER 36: r ...which is appropriate here?

CUSTOMER 35: or r with a circle... registered trademark... yeah

CUSTOMER 36: the r with a circle... oh nice... yeah, good suggestion Tim... I like it

CUSTOMER 35: I'm gonna be on the payroll soon

ROB: ...and that is some payroll

CUSTOMER 35: will work for oatmeal cookie

ROB: you're gonna be on the buttered roll... ha-ha

CUSTOMER 36: marijuana

ROB: marijuana

CUSTOMER 36: yeah

CUSTOMER 35: can he spell it?

ROB: m-a-r-i-j-i-u-a

CUSTOMER 36: j-u-a-n a

ROB: j-u-a-n a … all right

CUSTOMER 36: I would like a suggestion for a word that represents the pop culture interests of Coco's generation because I'm not in a position to know what those are and you are

ROB: a, uh, an iconogra… an i…

CUSTOMER 36: …like an iconic pop culture word for Coco's generation

ROB: you mean a person?… you mean like a phrase?..

CUSTOMER 36: it could be anything… just a single word that you think really captures an important aspect of that generation's engagement with pop culture

ROB: you want me to tell you first of just write it?

CUSTOMER 36: let's talk a bit

ROB: I like i-l-y-y

CUSTOMER 36: what's that?

ROB: "I love you" with an extra y

CUSTOMER 36: that's perfect!… I think that's great, I love it!

ROB: I don't really, you know…

CUSTOMER 37: [inaudible]

ROB: yeah, i-l-y-y

CUSTOMER 35: "I love you you"

CUSTOMER 38: so the y-y is the normal...?

ROB: just extra

CUSTOMER 37: "I love you you"

CUSTOMER 36: it's very puzzling, i-l-y-y

CUSTOMER 35: "I love your you"...

CUSTOMER 36: yeah that's nice, i-l-y-y

CUSTOMER 35: you guys know what that is

CUSTOMER 38 [OFF]: I just heard what he said... yeah, right...

CUSTOMER 35: I never use that... now I'm gonna use that...

ROB: see you're not twelve... if you were twelve years old you'd know all about that

CUSTOMER 35: Coco texts me all day

CUSTOMER 36: and then the last one...

ROB: the last one... all day, all night?

CUSTOMER 35: really?

CUSTOMER 36: ...is an internet acronym...

ROB: ...a lot... yeah

CUSTOMER 36: it's capital T, l, semicolon, d, r with no space

ROB: mm-hmm... Tl;dr... look right?

CUSTOMER 36: does it look good?

ROB: or do you want it thinner?

CUSTOMER 36: I think thinner maybe... yeah... so it looks more type-y

CUSTOMER 39 [OFF]: no I don't have a T930... this thing is so old

CUSTOMER 36: that's perfect, yeah, that's just right

CUSTOMER 35 [OFF]: you can't turn that thing on

CUSTOMER 38 [OFF]: the T9?

CUSTOMER 35 [OFF]: the ability to predict... you type two things and it will give you the word

CUSTOMER 36: fabulous

ROB: that's it?

CUSTOMER 36: that's it

ROB: fantastic... ok, now...

CUSTOMER 35: can I take this opportunity now to go out?...

CUSTOMER 36: skedaddle

CUSTOMER 35: ...go on a date with your secretary who I've been busy courting

Customers 37, 38, 39

CUSTOMER 37: hi self... um... I have one word... I only have one

ROB: ok

CUSTOMER 37: I would like ampersand

ROB: mm-hmm

CUSTOMER 37: ...with these

ROB: written on that?

CUSTOMER 37: no I want an a, an m, and a p

ROB: all on those blocks?... oh, I don't [inaudible]...

CUSTOMER 37: ok

ROB: oh, I'm sorry

CUSTOMER 37: no that's ok, I just thought of that when you showed me these

ROB: I don't have...

CUSTOMER 37: ...oooh

ROB: yeah, yeah, I don't... I have a few of those...

CUSTOMER 37: ok... so, um, then maybe I would just like... I don't know... [off] hey, he doesn't have enough to make these

ROB: I don't have a full alphabet... uh...

CUSTOMER 36: oh, what else do you need... what about... what else did you want?

CUSTOMER 37: I wanted ampersand

CUSTOMER 36: oh... and he doesn't have an ampersand?... can't he just put an ampersand on it?

CUSTOMER 37: no, no, no, no, no... he doesn't have the letters to spell it out

ROB: I don't have the letters to spell it out

CUSTOMER 36: hmm...

CUSTOMER 37: uh-oh... am I your first disappointment?

ROB: but I have a... um...

CUSTOMER 37: I'm thinking… um… of an alternative

CUSTOMER 36: what if… what if he took the letters that he does have?… do you have a lot of the letters?

ROB: I might… I mean it would take… to give you a sense… to do that (pointing to signage) took me an hour

CUSTOMER 37: right

ROB: so we could go through and find out… it would take over an hour to do it…

CUSTOMER 37: I don't even want you to color them in

ROB: it doesn't matter, it would take an hour… you have to line 'em up and you have to do the…

CUSTOMER 36: I think… don't you want those actual objects?

CUSTOMER 37: I want the objects

ROB: oh you don't want…

CUSTOMER 37: I want this (holding up a letter stencil)

ROB: them… actually… done?

CUSTOMER 37: nope

ROB: you want the actual… well, let's see what we got

CUSTOMER 37: is that ok?

ROB: I know we don't have all of them… absolutely…

CUSTOMER 37: I'm taking your material

CUSTOMER 36: maybe what he could do is, he could write the missing letters

CUSTOMER 37: but you are closing soon

ROB: I would love to give you...

CUSTOMER 37: ...everything must go

ROB: ...I would love to give you all these

CUSTOMER 36: you know, if it was like b, a ...but he didn't have the a then maybe he could write the a there?

CUSTOMER 37: see, I don't know

CUSTOMER 36: ...and he could just put the next letter next to it...

CUSTOMER 37: see I don't know if that would be interesting

ROB: all I know...

CUSTOMER 37: ...see what we have...

ROB: if I have the whole alphabet...

CUSTOMER 37: right and there's some repetition... who knows what that's like? ok... a...

ROB: here! here is the ampersand itself!

CUSTOMER 37: maybe I should just take that?

ROB: that's, uh...

CUSTOMER 37: I could just take that

ROB: no you should get what you want

CUSTOMER 38: did you make these stencils or were they prefab?

ROB: no I bought them

CUSTOMER 37: you're running low on battery power by the way so I don't know if you have a plug...

ROB: I don't, uh, do I?... wow... I had no idea I would be so busy...

CUSTOMER 37: the last day, it's a closeout

ROB: um... ok, while we're doing that, could I take care of somebody else?

CUSTOMER 37: yes

ROB: ok, 'cause this will be a little while

CUSTOMER 37: ok

ROB: ...and I can take care of you

CUSTOMER 37: they were in front of me, so I don't know if they wanna...

ROB: are you guys ready?

CUSTOMER 37: you guys ready?

ROB: you guys are ready? yeah? all right good... let's see what I got here in terms of battery... very little... I'll just do as much as I can, ok? ok, I'm Rob, who are you?

CUSTOMER 38: I'm Julie

ROB: hi

CUSTOMER 38: hi

ROB: how do you know about the word shop?

CUSTOMER 38: well he had sent me the link and also...

ROB: ...what's your name?

CUSTOMER 39: Dax

ROB: hi

CUSTOMER 39: hi

CUSTOMER 38: ...he sent me the link, but then also we saw your reading yesterday night

ROB: oh, great

CUSTOMER 38: and, um, yeah

ROB: so here you are at Rob's Word Shop... so happy... ok, so by now you kinda got a sense of how this all works?

CUSTOMER 38: yeah

ROB: all right... excellent... um, all right... good... and what, what are you thinking?

CUSTOMER 38: um... what words?

ROB: yeah, or... yeah... words... or if you want you can have a word

CUSTOMER 38: I have some words and I also have some punctuation

ROB: beautiful... punctuation's free by the way

CUSTOMER 38: oh... ok

ROB: what a steal... knock yourself out with the punctuation... yeah

CUSTOMER 38: ok... ok, well I guess first and foremost I want a colon

ROB: you want a colon... ok...

CUSTOMER 38: yeah

ROB: everybody needs a colon... ok... marker?

CUSTOMER 38: yeah that's fine

ROB: is that good?

CUSTOMER 38: that's perfect

ROB: all right, so one colon... that's gonna be free of charge... all right, colon...

CUSTOMER 38: um… an ampersand

ROB: they're popular

CUSTOMER 38: are they?

CUSTOMER 37 [OFF]: that's what I'm doing… I want ampersand as my word

CUSTOMER 38: oh wow [inaudible]

ROB: great minds think alike

CUSTOMER 38: and can I have the word through?… is it possible to have it go across two sheets of paper though?

ROB: go across?

CUSTOMER 38: like two sheets of paper… so, like, if you write it just like big across two…

ROB: yeah… I even have a piece of tape

CUSTOMER 38: oh, yeah, that would be good

ROB: all right now, um, this is gonna be the end of the videotaping I'm afraid…

APPENDIX

Caveat Lector; or, Reference as Pig in a Poke

> "An author who is writing specifically for a public is not really writing: it is the public that is writing, and for this reason the public can no longer be a reader; reading only appears to exist. This is why works created to be read are meaningless: no one reads them. This is why it is dangerous to write for other people, in order to evoke the speech of others and reveal them to themselves: the fact is that other people do not want to hear their own voices; they want to hear someone else's voice, a voice that is read, profound, troubling like the truth."
> —Maurice Blanchot

Everything takes place twice, in a logical (but not necessarily temporal) sequence. First as intention and second as disposition. First as product and second as fallout. Any intentional act is accompanied by innumerable byproducts. Every process of production creates byproducts that it did not intend to create yet cannot help but slough off and which do not factor into the final product (except obliquely), and are therefore useless—but necessarily so. In general, any process is the division of a given in two: a use and a useless share. Language, for instance, is a process that divides a given range of sound into meaningful and meaningless utterances. A religious process may divide a given human body into pure and impure parts, holy and profane behaviors. Of course, this is not to imply that what I am calling a "given" or "given body" is an originary and pure value that is subsequently defiled by secondary processes. What is given to one process is the product of another. 'Given,' 'process,' and 'product' are three appearances of an ideal and therefore impossible object. In fact, the first act of any process is to define for itself what is given it, and it does this through a sort of creative recognition (or misrecognition), since it is itself indistinct from the process it performs on the given body of its unconscious choice. An industrial process is given a set of inputs, which it divides into those that are useful, that end up part of the final product, and those that are useless, becoming waste or byproduct. A worker is a good example of byproduct: it is fed and cared for as long as it is useful for the creation of surplus value and then disposed of as waste once it becomes useless (e.g., sick, old, disabled).

Intention defines the regime of the process, and product, its purpose. For example, I intend to write an essay on Rob's Word Shop, and my product is this essay. Disposition (an archival term for the fate of a record: shelf or shredder) defines other external processes that feed or feed off of the process in question—it describes how other processes are related to the process in question. Fallout is the share of the given that must be excised in order for the intentional process to identify itself *as intention* by identifying with its product and not with the entire given, which it retains as ground or alibi. In this way, fallout always bears the mark of the process from which it is ejected, and this mark may come to circulate in other processes despite its uselessness to the initial process (beyond supporting its identity by its exclusion).

[what the fuck does this even mean?]

The Word Shop was a process like any other. Its intention was the production of objects bearing words and letters, which were its products. Its disposition included office supplies, which supported the process, and video and transcripts of each sale, which have gone on to feed a secondary process, the creation of this book. The carbon copies of receipts, for example, are part of the fallout of this process—byproducts that bear the marks of the primary products and processes but are not themselves included in the set of those products.

This portion of the book is about fallout, about waste, and its purpose is to supplement the transcripts of the transactions, which the book has brought out from under the sign of disposition and placed under the domain of intention. We can see that the book and the shop have played musical chairs with our four registers: The book takes the place of product, and the Word Shop itself becomes disposition. This essay will take its place opposite the book under the sign of fallout. As a reading, as a secondary product of the book, this essay will remain a necessary evil incommensurable to the product that repels it.

Rob's Word Shop was first a shop disguised as an art project housed in the front window of the Bowery Poetry Club, Tuesdays through Thursdays from 11 to 2 PM beginning May 5, 2010 and ending twenty-two days later. At the shop, customers, mostly friends or friends of friends, bought words or letters that Rob printed—by hand or with the aid of a printer—for a set amount. It is only now, years later, a book.

I don't remember when Rob asked me to take part in the project—there is no record of the invitation, so I assume it was a verbal one. I was twenty-nine at the time, which seems to me now a long time ago, but that's just the product of a poor memory sprinkled with nostalgia and a just a dollop of regret. I was working part-time as an archivist at NYU's special collections library, so Rob (who'd helped me land the job in the first place), looking to document what was essentially an ephemeral, time-based piece, and in keeping with the theme of the project, asked me to be his records manager.

The story of Rob setting up shop and me helping out while useful to any understanding of the book is not sufficient to exhaust the 'significance' of the book. The relation between the shop and this book is not one of reality and representation, not one of fact and repetition, not even one of event and remainder. The shop and the book are essentially independent of one another. It's true that the two have a temporal sequence; there's no use in denying that. After all, one can't father one's own mother no matter how much she'd like that.

Logically, the two are related, not joined by a relationship of original and copy, but instead by a shared referent posited after the fact as something suddenly recognized as having been the absent reason for the project in the first place, in so far as the project has taken the twin paths of shop and book. This shared referent would be the definition of the given discussed above, in that it is as much produced as it is suffered. Neither product nor fallout, neither intention nor disposition, this referent remains at the center of the four domains of process even as we shift from shop to book, from receipt book to essay.

The product of the word shop exists as a set of leaves of paper marked with ink, first and final intention of our writer-entrepreneur: It is finally a commodity. The fallout is a set of evidences, produced unconsciously, documenting the shop—evidences that are either memories etched in the axons of customers' brains or in the records and office supplies accumulated during the process (albeit with an eye towards making a book). The book is a record of those records—of the product and fallout—and so attempts to occupy a space that is neither the information contained herein nor the traces of its production. For now, we will assign to this space irreducible to both the information compiled herein and to the process of its production the name "the Book," since it is the form of the book that defines the dominion and the central object of interpretation.

The Book is a writing of neither the product nor the fallout. The disposed fallout organizes itself by an immanent logic into an archive. The Book does not participate in the reciprocal substitution of primary and secondary sources. The book is perhaps the locus of that exchange itself, *post factum, post festum*.

We've said that the Book is a referent that the book and the Word Shop share. We can see that its relation to both is one of withdrawal. Neither the book you hold in your hands nor the performance that occasioned it, this referent remains mute and insignificant—it does not circulate, it provides no testimony or alibi. This unnamable is no longer legible; in fact, it was never legible. To speak of it, we would have to forget, actively, the product and the fallout, the collated and distributed book and the body of archival evidence. And this is key: We can say, This is why the Word Shop happened (its cause), or, This is what the Word Shop produced (its end), but never both statements at the same time.

Of course, we are capable of discussing the material forces that converged to form the Word Shop, that is, we are able to explain the Word Shop as a social phenomenon, but only if we take the Word Shop to be merely the sum of those forces. But to understand the Word Shop in this way is to preclude any possibility of engaging with the Word Shop as something that escapes, if only partially, the determinations of its material investments—that is, as something other than just what was. One could ask, "Who's to say that it wasn't just the sum total of its social effects or phenomenal appearances?" No one, certainly. One has to wager on the existence of that third *something*—a wager that may come to be itself that very thing. Is this *thing*, the referent, unique to *this* book? Is it a property of *all* books? Is this book one of only a select few that manifests this *something else?* I'd wager it's a little of all three. And it will be my contention that this wager belongs to the reader, to those who are forced by happenstance to reckon with this book, really any book, and construct, again and again, the Book absent from all shelves.

This insignificant referent that is illegibly reinscribed in the Book appears as mute fact because it is what finally cannot be reduced to conditions nor decomposed into larger or more basic cultural processes without abandoning the object of inquiry altogether, an absurdity since this critical decomposition would render void the very object that inspired its interrogation in the first place. It is, finally, the banal particularity of its existence. One is forced to accept this irreducible kernel as meaningless remainder or assent to the ultimate absurdity and self-contradiction of the enterprise of critical investigation, which produces results at the cost of consistency. It is possible to conceive of this mute fact as a product of this very impasse, a *trompe l'oeil* brought about by the inconsistency of interpretation. In that case, the rational move would be to accept the groundlessness of interpretation and assent to an absolute relativization that signals the end of history. This characterizes the contemporary conjuncture of nihilistic apathy, of postmodern relativism. Against the capitulation to postmodern relativity, to insist on the existence of the irreducible and insignificant kernel is to inaugurate a thinking that is neither the critical hermeneutics of the nihilist nor the genetic fallacy of the reactionary.

The partial archive of receipt books presented here (and what archive is impartial?) is essentially a testimony to the simultaneous presence and non-presence of the Word Shop, its existence as the sum of its material relations and its retirement into the inconsistency of that *summa*. I say "essentially" because this testimony is not subject to interpretation; it will not allow itself to be reduced to a consistent set of statements about the Word Shop. And yet, it demands a response, demands responsibility, demands interpretations. And it does so precisely because no response, in the end, will do.

The book, *this* book, joins intention and product to disposition and fallout; it joins the whole swirl of words and letters and time sheets and rubber stamps *out there* to the transcripts and photographic reproductions *in here*. It does this because it draws as near as possible to, without coinciding with, an unassimilable fact—a fact which by definition is immediate and absolutely present and therefore inaccessible to us. This book, while detailing the conversations between Rob and his customers, is yet not about the buying and selling of words. It is not a history of the Word Shop—it only obliquely touches on that project, culling together as it does the fallout of those many exchanges, and in that obliqueness its referent never coincides completely with that of the Word Shop. What it is *about* is the fact of the Book, the fact of any book, charting its adventure through the world, divulging its secrets to anyone whosoever.

Any book is the Book if it anticipates for the reader the singular contingency of its production to become absolute, if it is able to signal that contingency in a silent language that does not immediately decompose the order in which its speech is legible.

Not every book exists as a sign of it's own insignificant origin, the ultimate insufficiency of any provenance, but every book exists because of the possibility of becoming such a sign. That is for the very simple reason that every book is finally unreadable—any book if not **nearly** unreadable (like, say, the Voynich manuscript) is at the very least irreducible to interpretation. The potential for a book to coincide with the Book has nothing to do with the death of the author, with the refutation of realism and naïve representation, or with the obliteration of a book's provenance—a book that is nothing other than the exposition of its composition is as exposed to contingency as, say, Homer's *Iliad*, a text that can't help but advertise its lack of pedigree. There are an infinite number of ways of exposing this unexpositable exposure of a book to the immediacy of its own history. This is true for anything at all—to be is to be exposed to this intimate immediacy. It is only because history takes the form of exposition that the Book **as a form** is exemplary. To mark a page is already to have crossed out the silence indistinguishable from an clamor. In this way, the Book is a kind of crease in Being.

That is all to say that what I am calling 'the Book,' the insistence of dumb fact in writing, is neither an innovative compositional technique nor a novel hermeneutical theory.

Every book is equally unfinished. Thus each is equally open to a subject that is neither author nor critic. A book may miss its referent, may not evoke the occasion that it names; it is not any less open for that, only misdirected, too near or too far. This has nothing to do with knowledge—especially not a lack of knowledge (or know-how) on the part of the reader (or the writer for that matter). Knowledge hasn't even entered the picture. With these 'unfortunate' books—those literally 'without chance'—one can always *interpret* them, that is, reduce them to their determinations, at least enough to satisfy curiosity. And that's fine. It's quite possible to interpret *every* book, since every book is also an empty sign of testimony itself, the structural vocative that accompanies any mark that has even the semblance of intention. That is why a book can be interpreted at all.

So, the incompleteness of any book, while true, is banal. With books that to a greater or lesser extent bear the mark of their contingency, the reader does not escape the book in the form of a critical transcendence or a totalizing contextualization that thinks its way out of the so-called imaginary capture of '*mere* reading' or 'reading for pleasure.' Instead, the Book, and in particular the insignificant referent to which it silently testifies, overcomes the reader—the Book that is to become. These fortunate books produce the interpretation as product and the interpreter as fallout. The insignificant referent, the third-order precipitate, escapes this back-and-forth in order to reproduce itself infinitely as an index, as pure deixis. Reading is not something readers do *with* texts or *to* texts. Reading is an occasion for encounters between things of which the reader—the solitary, contemplative reader—is but one among many. This process is possible because the referent continually absents itself, and the distance between the insignificant referent and the Book that writes itself around it, is the field of reading as an articulation of the abstract and the concrete.

To come to terms with the relations of product, fallout, and referent is already to abandon the project as unproductive of the radicalization of writing. It is no longer imperative that we change writing through experimentation and innovation but that we change reading. Or, if we do not change reading, that allow reading to take place. That is to say, reading has not begun to write its own history, and the history that writing has produced has functioned to delay that of reading. Writing suffers from poor reading because all writing is the fallout of a prior reading. And in so far as the so-called innovative forms of writing claims the power to 'liberate' its readership via a didactic radicalism, those forms of writing will disallow reading, especially the readings that those forms of writing already in so far as they are in turn inscriptive fallout. Only a writing indifferent to its readings could persist in the partiality of its testimony. The same be said for any of writing (or art for that matter) that styles itself as participatory or relational or as 'social practice' 'in order,' writes Blanchot, 'to evoke the speech of others and reveal them to themselves.' To stage writing as an orthopedic curriculum is to succumb to an authoritarian disaster.

At the same time, to say that writing is already a form of reading (i.e., its fallout), does not give us permission to champion so-called accessible writing over more-artificial or formally unfamiliar modes. There is no normal mode of writing, no audience in the singular. This dress-pattern conformity in our time is nothing more than the inescapable expression of the institutional nature of creative writing programs.

Even so, the political character of the defenders of accessibility is one of irresponsible conformism whose alibi is the liberal fantasy of the free market (to the extent that its corruption and coercion are suppressed). To stage writing as a form of economic exchange is to characterize it as a mode of supply and demand, where the reader always gets what she came for.

Instead, in terms of the Book, the reader never gets what she came for. The Book is not one—one reading, one meaning, one text—but neither is it the sum (as if it could be calculated) of all the material conditions that preceded as well as social and technological contexts that surround the composition of the Book (whether in its production or its reception). To understand the singular but by no means unitary space that the Book carves out for itself between indivisibility and multiplicity, I will now focus my attention on the process of reference and the nature of the insignificant referent, which I will refer to as the "insignified."

The process of reference, which reaches beyond the confines of the book toward the guarantor of its meaning, is infinitized by the insignified of the Book. The Book takes the division of inside and outside as its subject, but it does so obliquely and without representing that to a reader, otherwise it would risk producing that division as another meaning circulating in a regime ruled by a different division.

What does the book refer? We can easily discover what the text refers to. We can say, "That word means this," and, "This word means that." But we cannot say to what the book refers, except, perhaps, using a cryptic phrase, the 'event of its com-position.'

Any book is the fallout of a singular productive encounter captured by the book. The referent is a necessary (though, not in itself necessary) jumping-off point for a new adventure, the adventure of the Book. What I have come to calling the "insignified" is not a fullness of meaning that comes to the rescue of any invariably partial interpretation. The insignified is first of all the phantasmal alibi for all meaning—the insignified assures us of the correct meaning of a text only as long as we don't scrutinize it, that we don't actually interrogate the validity of its claims. In terms of its role as alibi, its existence and not its authority is sufficient. This brings us to our second point, which is that the insignified is also the very process of a text's deference to its authority. The presumption of inscrutability is based upon the prohibition on interrogation, which is in turn grounded in the structural necessity of the insignified as referent to any communication of meaning. There is no violence in the establishment of this authority—its authority is premised on the structural impossibility of interrogating it within the system that it organizes as referent. The system of meaning upheld by the insignified forbids any interrogation of the referent because such interrogation is impossible. The authority of the insignified is a byproduct of its structural inscrutability. As soon as one interrogates it, it is no longer the referent one wished to interrogate. The once-inscrutable referent is now just a sign in another system with its own inscrutable insignified—the meaning of the now-interrogated referent is in part a function of a new and necessarily inscrutable insignified. The function of reference can never become a subject of discourse.

This referent is insignificant. Without significance, it operates precisely to the extent that it is unnamable. Were we to name it, regardless of whether that be possible, it would no longer function. In naming

230

this referent, which I refer to as the 'insignified,' we enter into another order of meaning, absolutely cut off from the previous order, bounded as it was by the now-named referent that circulated in silence. Only another order of meaning could name what for the order in question is unnamable, and still, it could never name it *as* unnamable. The insignified is unnamable *only for the order it operates*. And for that reason it exists *in operation* only in that order. If we were to tease out all of the determinations and references of *this book*, if we were totally to contextualize, explain, and *interpret* it, we would never find the insignified that operates it. We would be left with an archive, an archive of the book we interpreted, but not the archive that our interpretation would produce as fallout, the archive that would chart the path of an exceptional referent.

The oneness of any book is tenuous, based as it is on a phantasmal relation to its referent, but this relationship cannot be explained away since the nature of the referent is one of mute fact. In the act of reference, the history of the referent is obscured. That history is itself the obfuscated history of a (logically) prior reference. Each referent was once a book, and any book is *one* because it has at least one other, its referent. Its referent appears to it *as* referent (and not as *book*) because the referent is for it the whole within which it is one. But that referent *is* only because it is, in its own right, a book with its *own* referent, its own other, which for the first book is inaccessible. This second-degree illegibility is a kind of protective *epoché*, a defensive suspension of infinite regression. A book has only the *fact* of its referent, *that* it exists or existed, but never the supposed plenitude of its full presence, which would be only lead to the infinite regress of reference. Not only must the referent be abandoned, but also it is already abandoned as mute fact in a defensive suspension of judgment that serves to protect that kernel whose exposure to a threatening contingency is its greatest strength.

But interpretation can be liberating (though maybe in a less immediately gratifying appearance) when it insists on a name for the insignified, to put it on trial, to testify to its irrepressible existence. But in that act, as discussed above, one risks transitioning into another order, the order in which our referent would then circulate meaningfully in a system structured around its own unspeakable referent. In that case, one would be right back where one started. One would have missed entirely the referent as enigmatic operator, instead reifying it in its materiality as the essential kernel of the system laid bare. But the kernel laid bare is not the kernel *in operando*. This, in any case, is the decision—between, on the one hand, a network theory of dispositions and positivitites and, on the other, a science of exceptions and the reinscription of the name of the proscribed.

The archive is the name for this deferential structure in its naïve state—testimony of an irretrievable history, attaining a completeness and fullness of meaning by failing to include within its anything that might suggest what has been left out or expunged. Like the memorial that it is, the very existence of an archive obscures the history it is supposed to make present—by offering its meager evidences, it successfully distracts one from the otherwise of an inaccessible history, and it does this by positing a history "out there" and "back then," when in fact both are simply perspectival projections of a flat anamorphosis. History would then be just another figure circulating in an absolute present. In this way, a book is an archive in the sense that its illusory completeness cannot be overcome by reference to external conditions, since it is itself an index of that supposedly vindicative outside.

A archives all the way down. Archives of archives, archives that archive each other's insignifieds. The Word Shop and this book are both archives, and yet they do not share the insignifieds that operate them respectively. The stack of illegibly palimpsested carbon copies, the time stamp and time card, and the other tokens of the workweek—all of these irreplaceable objects are gathered together by an archive whose founding gesture is the indifferent withdrawal of its occasion. But the archive is for that reason nothing special—it's just what is, a banality. Like this very book, the Word Shop bound together a variety of interests and desires, institutions and processes. Some were latent, others indifferent, but the Word Shop produced and signified a provisional and improvised assemblage of these more-or-less exclusive points of entry and lines of flight.

Some books, some archives, can be entirely decomposed into the interests and forces that operate them from without—their insignifieds either disappearing into the ether or attaining a kind of angelic fullness. We've reserved the name "the Book" for that which disappears under any attempt to reinscribe its manifold limits within some supposedly larger and more explanatory discursive structure. To be something other than a text, than an archive of archives, the Book must operate under the assumption that the gap separating intention and disposition, product and fallout, is something positive yet illegal, real yet interdicted. To posit the reality of the insignified and to read the system it organizes by its exclusion as an inverted form of its true message—this is a risk, a risk that can only be met by the autonomous coming-to-be of what could not have been said. This is the true meaning of reading—to attend, to await, rather, to tend to the production of that could not have been and assume illegally the means to do so, because this 'could not have been' in fundamentally distinct from the 'will have been' of an anticipatory nihilism.

May we then possibly reinscribe the insignified in the system it operates? Would that necessarily be to anticipate a fullness of meaning in the promise of a referent-to-come, only this time to appear within the text instead of outside of it? Instead, we, as writers and readers, must focus our efforts on the operation that produces the referent as a phantasmal but not therefore illusory figure of its own impossibility. It is via the structure of the referent's promise of meaning-to-come that the insignified might begin to warp the field of its silent operation. Any text is the organization of both the lack of meaning and the insatiable drive for closure. Unlike the anticipatory structure of the referent's promise, an operation on the operation of reference would imply a politics without a utopian flavor, one that projects this anticipatory structure as an infinite series of exceptions historicized as a duty toward the work of the work.

Only by turning the disposition and the fallout of the Word Shop into a book, do the purchases of an illiterate public become a text for the production of an agonistic community of readers. A reader is not an end-user in the way a customer is a non-reseller, that included exclusion that grounds the logic of commerce and bears the brunt of authorizing its apotheosis via their sole recognizable affect: satisfaction. Having turned its readers into writers (how very langpo!), the Word Shop was then able to convert the detritus of that awful process into a book that disentangles reading from consuming, that allows a moment of self-reflection from which the reader is obliged to escape or forego altogether. Only a reader writes, and only a reader of books writes the Book.

The Book, the book that demands to become, is not one; it gets carried away with each reader and rewritten with each reading. It is a speculative superposition of exclusive, overlapping, and contradictory encounters. Some encounters will be readings; others, interpretations—but the Book will never coincide with a single one of them.

Is this a book that participates in the coming-to-be of the Book? It is impossible to say. The structural elements described in this essay are not criteria for making value judgments. The proof of the Book is in the reading of it. Like each leaf, each letter, of the Book, the products of Rob's Word Shop carry on independently of anyone's intentions. The traces it leaves persist and are taken up by new processes, different orders, compassionate and antagonistic labors—this book being one of many uses to which the products of the Word Shop have been put. This brief essay itself takes part in that adventure insofar as it too wanders freely—written as it is by someone other than Rob Fitterman, for other purposes, representing yet another misuse of the Word Shop's records. This essay is fallout. It wishes to be more than *a* reading; it is driven to attempt an explication of the possibilities of reading based on a reading of the Word Shop. It is able to torque the field in which it is composed because it too is intention and product, it too is unfinished—glaringly so!

But the essay is also part of the book, bound by glue and technology and labor, and the book just is. You approach it as a given, regardless of its tortuous emergence. You will love it for a time, and then you will set it aside. It does not enter history at any one point. Over and over, it enters the histories that we produce as readers reading, and it does so wherever and whenever it can, wherever and whenever it does. Like the Word Shop, this very book assembles under its hastily raised banner whatever documents it could get its hands on that supported the labor of its undocumented insignified. Should this essay attempt to signify that guarded little sign? Should it signify its 'own' insignified even? Isn't that the very imperative of a paradoxically identitarian postmodernism and how it issues its cynical commands from the safety of the far side of its own sadistic logic? I leave the laying bear to you, hypocrite reader. I am not afraid of my insignified, I am faithful it will prevent any reading from lapsing into an infinitude of interpretations. That's the very least my insignified could have wanted—that it functioned at all. I can only be faithful to my intention. The fallout falls to the reader, to do with it whatever she wishes to the extent that her insignified functions (or malfunctions) at all as well.

631303

CUSTOMER'S ORDER NO.			DATE			
NAME						
ADDRESS						
CITY, STATE, ZIP						
SOLD BY	CASH	C.O.D.	CHARGE	ON ACCT.	MDSE RETD.	PAID OUT

QUAN.	DESCRIPTION	AMOUNT
1	4 WORD	1 20
2	2 LETTERS	1 —
3		
4		
5		
6		
7		
8		
9		
10		
11		
12		1 08
RECEIVED BY		

3705 **KEEP THIS SLIP FOR REFERENCE**

CUSTOMER'S ORDER NO.			DATE 3/19/200				
NAME							
ADDRESS							
CITY, STATE, ZIP							
SOLD BY	CASH	C.O.D.	CHARGE	ON ACCT.	MDSE RETD.	PAID OUT	

QUAN.	DESCRIPTION	AMOUNT
1	1 Quotation Marks	
2	" (gratis)	
3	"	
4	4 pages	
5		
6		
7		
8		
9		
10		
11		
12		3.00
RECEIVED BY		

3705 **KEEP THIS SLIP FOR REFERENCE**

CUSTOMER'S ORDER NO.	DATE	3/19/10

631346

SOLD BY	CASH	C.O.D.	CHARGE	ON ACCT.	MDSE RETD.	PAID OUT

QUAN.	DESCRIPTION	AMOUNT
1	wheels	
2	— pelican	
3	— ice	
4	— flowers	
5	— oil'd (grass)	
6		
7		
8		
9		
10		
11		
12		

RECEIVED BY

3705 KEEP THIS SLIP FOR REFERENCE

		631345

CUSTOMER'S ORDER NO.				DATE 5/19/00			
NAME							
ADDRESS							
CITY, STATE, ZIP							
SOLD BY	CASH	C.O.D.	CHARGE	ON ACCT.	MDSE RETD.	PAID OUT	

	QUAN.	DESCRIPTION	AMOUNT
1	3	words	3 00
2		— pelican	
3		— iceue	
4		— flowers	
5		— oil'd (gratis)	
6			
7			
8			
9			
10			
11			
12			3 00

RECEIVED BY

3705 **KEEP THIS SLIP FOR REFERENCE**

NO.	324853							
NAME: (CONT.)							DATE: 3/24/10	
ADDRESS:								
CITY, STATE, ZIP								
SOLD BY:		CASH	C.O.D.	CHARGE	ON ACCT.	MDSE RTD.	PAID OUT	

QUAN.		DESCRIPTION	AMOUNT
1½	1	WORD	1 50
	2	" DAUGHTER "	2 00
1	3	WORD	1 00
	4	" LAMPPOST "	
1	5	WORD	1 00
	6	" BOTTLE "	1 00
1	7	WORD	1 00
	8	" BABY "	
✓	9	WORD	1 00
	10	" BOYFRIEND "	
✓	11	WORD	1 00
	12	" THE "	FREE

CUSTOMER'S ORDER NO.   RECEIVED BY: 6 P

KEEP THIS COPY FOR YOUR RECORDS
5L240 ©2001 REDIFORM®